¡TACO LOCO!

MEXICAN STREET FOOD FROM SCRATCH

PAVILION

By Jonas Cramby **Photography by** Calle Stoltz

CONTENTS

FOREWORD

To travel to Mexico and eat only at the tourist resorts and beach restaurants is a bit like visiting the Louvre just to admire the no-smoking signs. Why? Because in Mexico, snacking has been elevated to an art form. Along every street, from little holes in the wall to the chaotic city mercados, you will find people hunched over disposable plates enjoying their favourite snack foods bought from one of the local street vendors. Lunch is usually a sit-down meal, but the rest of the day is set aside for snacking. Even if you're new in town it's easy to find local gems. Just follow these golden rules:

1 Choose the place with the largest crowd of people.

2 Make sure the person handling the money isn't the same as the one preparing the food.

3 Order a single taco, tostada or flauta – and only if it's good, order another one. Failing that, continue your excursion through the streets and one of the world's most unexplored street-food cuisines. Because even for those familiar with Mexican food, there is always something new to discover.

❋ ❋ ❋

First of all, the sheer breadth of choice is breathtaking. You could spend a whole holiday in just one of Mexico City's enormous mercados and still discover something new every day. When we think of Mexican food it's usually the more overloaded American version that springs to mind. If Tex-Mex food can be compared to one of Jeff Koons' over-sized balloon animal sculptures, genuine Mexican food is more like a minimalist concrete cube by Donald Judd. It's balanced, original and emotional. Most dishes consist of a simple filling, a quick salsa and a few carefully prepared corn tortillas. It's more about care and flavour balance than expensive ingredients and complicated preparation methods. And that's why the food also works so well to cook at home.

❋ ❋ ❋

At least that was my initial thought as I started to write this book. The recipes are an attempt to recreate my Mexican street-food favourites in a home kitchen. I've written the recipes as simply as possible without cutting corners or sacrificing authenticity. Some dishes taste pretty much exactly as they do standing by a taqueria in Mexico City, while others, the barbacoa or the al pastor, for example, are variations adapted for a home kitchen without a rotisserie grill or smoke pit. They all have one thing in common, however: I'm certain that you will eat them with a glazed look in your eyes and a fire in your heart.

Jonas Cramby
Casa de Mezcal, Oaxaca

BÁSICOS

PART 1: TORTILLAS, SALSAS AND OTHER BASIC TECHNIQUES

Women in the village of Zaachila prepare corn tortillas on comales – traditional wood-fired flat griddles made from clay. Note the wheelbarrow with masa in the background. I want it!

TODO SOBRE LA TORTILLA

All about corn, wheat and nixtamal tortillas

Although Mexico is responsible for many of the world's tastiest foods – such as chocolate, tomatoes, peanuts, avocado, vanilla and chilli – it's corn and corn tortillas that lie at the heart of Mexican cuisine. Corn tortillas are either prepared from a ready-made mix, called *masa harina*, or from fresh *masa* (corn dough), which is commonly found in local tortillerías but which you can also make yourself at home. For those reluctant to give up their gluten, you can, of course, also bake wheat tortillas.

Tortillas are not made from standard cornmeal but from nixtamal, which is made by a simple, age-old process that has existed in Mexico since Anno Domini. Dried corn is boiled in limewater, then rinsed and ground into a dough that is either used straight away or dried to make *masa harina*. It's this nixtamalization process that contributes the characteristic tortilla flavour and increases the nutritional value beyond that of standard corn. It's even said that it was because of this that the Aztec and Maya could grow from small tribes into enormous empires while we in Northern Europe walked around in animal skins and spoke in monosyllables. If you want to make your own masa, however, there are a few things to keep in mind.

❀ **The corn** Unfortunately you can't use popcorn kernels when making fresh masa. However, almost all other kinds of corn work superbly – such as yellow, white or blue dried dent corn, flint corn or cornflour (cornstarch). You'll find them in South American food stores or online (see page 26).

❀ **The lime (calcium hydroxide)** The slaked lime used for nixtamalization is an alkaline and mildly corrosive, so be careful when handling it. Rinse the corn thoroughly and make sure you only buy food-grade slaked lime. 'Cal mexicana' and 'pickling lime' are two types that can be bought online, for example.

❀ **The mill** Traditionally a stone mill is used, but you can also use a blender or a corona mill, which is a hand-operated mill sold in home-brewing shops as a malt or grain mill. In that case, run the dough through three times to get the right consistency.

TORTILLAS MASA HARINA

Tortillas made from ready-made tortilla mix

MAKES 16

250g/9oz/2 cups masa harina, for example
   Maseca
about 250ml/9fl oz/1 cup water

1   The most popular way to prepare corn
    tortillas is to use masa harina, a ready-made
    tortilla mix that is blended with water. You'll
    find it in South American food stores or
    online (see page 26). However, you'll have to
    show some tender care. The dough needs to
    be perfectly wet, the tortilla thin enough and
    the temperature just right. You will also need
    a tortilla press and a clean plastic bag. Got
    all of these? Then let's get started. Put the
    flour in a bowl, gradually add the water and
    work into a dough, about 5 minutes. Cover
    and leave to rest for 5 minutes. Cut out two
    circles from a plastic bag the same size as
    your tortilla press and put one in the press.
    Shape a ping-pong-ball-size ball from the
    dough, place in the press and cover with
    the other plastic circle. Press, then rotate
    the tortilla 180 degrees and press again. It
    should be thin and even. If your tortilla tears
    at the edges, the dough is too dry. If it sticks
    to the plastic, it's too wet. Adjust with more
    water or flour as necessary. When the dough
    is just right, divide it into 16 equal parts, roll
    into balls and press as you go along.

2   Fry the tortillas in a dry frying pan that's
    a bit warmer than medium heat. The secret
    is to flip a tortilla after 20 seconds, then after
    45 seconds, then again after 45 seconds.
    Leave it to cook for a final 30 seconds until
    it's ready. The tortilla should have puffed up
    and be spotted brown but not be burned or
    hard. If it is, lower the heat. If it's pale, turn
    up the heat. Pile up the breads in a tortilla
    warmer as they're ready, or wrap them in a
    tea towel. This is to keep them warm and to
    make them soft and tender. Serve as soon as
    all the tortillas are fried.

TORTILLAS DE NIXTAMAL

Tortillas made from fresh masa

MAKES 30

250g/9oz/2 cups dried corn
1.7 litres/60fl oz/6⅔ cups water
1 tbsp cal mexicana
250g/9oz/2 cups masa harina
1 tsp salt

1   Making tortillas from fresh masa might seem
    complicated, but people make their own
    fresh pasta and that's far more complicated.
    Tortillas made from fresh masa taste much
    better than those made from masa harina.
    They become softer, taste fresher, have
    a higher nutritional content and will get
    a fantastic popcorn character when fried.
    To make fresh masa at home is one of those
    things that people on the internet claim
    is impossible without special equipment.
    Not true. All you need is a blender, preferably
    a powerful one like Vitamix, and one day's
    worth of forward planning. Got these? Then
    let's go!

At the local tortillería, the owner thoroughly rinses the corn, partly to get rid of any slaked lime but also to make sure the husk comes off properly.

2   Rinse your dried corn. Put it in a pan with 1.5 litres/2½ pints/6½ cups of the water and the cal mexicana. Slowly bring it to the boil over a medium heat, 30–45 minutes. Cover, remove from the heat and leave to stand at room temperature for at least 8 hours.

3   Rinse the corn in cold water for 5 minutes while rubbing between your fingers to remove the husks. Rinse, then cover with water and rest for 5 minutes. Rinse again.

4   Add half the corn to a blender with 100ml/3½fl oz/scant ½ cup water to make sure you get a smooth dough. If it feels a bit grainy, keep blending. Repeat with the other half. Now you'll end up with a masa that is too wet for frying, so knead in about 100g/3½oz/ heaped ¾ cup of masa harina with the salt. Cook according to the instructions for tortillas masa harina. Leftover dough can be kept in the refrigerator for up to 5 days.

TOSTADAS
Deep-fried corn tortillas

MAKES 20
20 ready-made corn tortillas
oil for deep-frying
salt

1   A tostada is a whole, round, deep-fried corn tortilla. In contrast to all the other tortilla varieties in this book, they're best when made from ready-made corn tortillas. Heat some oil in a frying pan – about 1 cm/¾in is enough. Test the temperature with a piece of corn tortilla – it should bubble as soon as you put it in the oil. Add one whole corn tortilla to the pan at a time and deep-fry, flipping over half way through, until it's crisp and golden yellow. Leave to drain on paper towels, then sprinkle with salt to serve.

TORTILLAS DE HARINA
Tortillas made from wheat flour

MAKES 20
350g/12oz/scant 3 cups plain (all-purpose) flour
1 tsp baking powder
1 tsp salt
50g/1¾oz butter or lard
250ml/9fl oz/1 cup warm water

1   Although corn tortillas are the most common, Mexicans eat wheat tortillas too, especially in the northern areas, possibly influenced by the neighbouring Tex-Mex culture. If you want a more animalistic, round, authentic Mexican flavour to your tortillas, use lard instead of butter – or tallow, as the Mexicans do. Mix the dry ingredients in a bowl. Work in the fat until you get a crumbly mix. Gradually add the warm water and work into a dough, about 5 minutes. Add more flour if the mixture is too wet.

2   Cover the dough and leave to rest for 20 minutes. Divide into 20 equal parts and roll into balls. Cover. Roll out one dough ball at a time while occasionally rotating it to make it circular. It should preferably be so thin that it's almost transparent.

3   Fry the tortillas in a dry frying pan heated to just a little warmer than medium heat. A tortilla that puffs up will be tastier – the secret is to flip it 3 times, first after 20 seconds, then after 45 seconds, then again after 45 seconds. Leave it to cook for a final 30 seconds until it's ready. The tortilla should have puffed up and be spotted brown but not be burned or hard. If it gets that way, lower the heat. If it's pale, turn up the heat. Pile up the breads in a tortilla warmer as they're ready, or wrap in a tea towel. This keeps them warm and makes them soft and tender. Serve as soon as all the tortillas are fried.

BRING HOME FROM MEXICO

These essentials should be on every traveller's shopping list.

Mezcal: Again, obviously, you'll want the classic Mexican drink.

Utensils: A lime press and other kitchen utensils like a tortilla press and a molcajete (mortar and pestle).

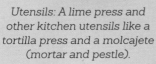

Sal de gusano: A mixture of salt, chilli and ground worms to sprinkle over your orange wedges when drinking mezcal.

Jícaras: Beautifully decorated bar bowls to drink mezcal from.

Chamoy sticks: Festive, sweet, tamarind-covered straws for micheladas.

Veladoras: Grave candles that are used for drinking mezcal from once burned out.

Mexican sweets: Obviously.

SALSAS Y CURTIDOS

Raw, chopped and roasted salsas and pickles

A really well-balanced salsa can bring sunshine on the cloudiest of days. It lights up the gloomiest of fillings, freshens up the driest of tortillas and ensures that everyone around your table has a smile on their face. Even though most of the salsas in this chapter are incredibly simple and take only a couple of minutes to prepare, there are a few small details you should keep in mind if you want to become a salsa king or queen.

❀ **The flavour balance** You really need to make use of your tastebuds when preparing salsa. The sizes of vegetables vary, so do the acidity levels in lime and the heat in chilli. The secret of a good salsa is the balance between these ingredients and salt. So use these recipes as a guide, but also trust your tastebuds.

❀ **The timing** The raw salsas on the following pages are easy to make in only a couple of minutes, so prepare them just before serving. The cooked salsas and pickles will take a little longer – ideally make them a day in advance to allow them time to cool and develop their flavours. If you're deciding which salsa to serve with tonight's taco, most salsas work with most things, but my favourites would be the classics: pico de gallo (see page 20), salsa cruda (see page 20) and salsa verde (see page 20) as a topping or as a dip.

❀ **The proportions** When you assemble the taco, don't use too much salsa; they're not salads and you're not eating according to the meat and two veg principle. At least not today. Instead, take a tortilla, add an embarrassingly large spoonful of filling, add one spoonful of salsa (just use one kind per taco) and sprinkle with some chopped coriander (cilantro) and white onion or sliced radishes for extra crunch. Take a bite and if you need more acidity/sweetness, perhaps you can add a squeeze of lime juice or some pickled onions; for more heat, add a few drops of chilli sauce; for more saltiness, crumble over some queso fresco. But remember, the filling is the star of the show. Of course, it's nice that the salsa dropped by to say hello, but it's really there to enhance the rest of the taco, celebrate it, laugh at its jokes and nod interestedly at its anecdotes. Okay?

SALSA VERDE

Tomatillo salsa

MAKES ABOUT 300G/10½OZ

1 bunch coriander (cilantro)
2–3 jalapeño peppers
½ white onion
1 garlic clove
250g/9oz tomatillos or physalis
lime (optional)
salt

1   Blend to a smooth salsa. Season to taste with salt and chilli. If you're using physalis, you might need to add a squeeze of lime.

SALSA CRUDA

Tomato salsa

MAKES ABOUT 500G/1LB 2OZ

400g/14oz canned plum tomatoes
juice of ½ lime
1 bunch coriander (cilantro)
2 garlic cloves
½ white onion
2–3 red chillies
salt

1   Blend the ingredients to a smooth salsa. Season to taste with salt, more lime and chilli.

SALSA DE AGUACATE

Tomatillo and avocado salsa

MAKES ABOUT 500G/1LB 2OZ

250g/9oz tomatillos or physalis, chopped
2 avocados, peeled, pitted and chopped
1 bunch coriander (cilantro), chopped
2–3 jalapeño peppers, deseeded and chopped
½ white onion, chopped
2 garlic cloves, chopped
a squeeze of lime (optional)
salt

1   Mix the ingredients and season to taste.

PICO DE PEPINO

Chopped cucumber salsa

MAKES ABOUT 300G/10½OZ

1 cucumber, peeled, deseeded and finely chopped
1 white onion, finely chopped
2–3 jalapeño peppers, deseeded and finely chopped
1 bunch coriander (cilantro) leaves, chopped
1 tbsp freshly squeezed lime juice
salt

1   Mix the ingredients and season to taste.

PICO DE GALLO

Chopped tomato salsa

MAKES ABOUT 300G/10½OZ

200g/7oz vine tomatoes, deseeded and chopped
1 white onion, finely chopped
1–2 jalapeño peppers, deseeded and chopped
1 bunch coriander (cilantro), chopped
2 tbsp freshly squeezed lime juice
salt

1   Mix the chopped ingredients together. Add the lime juice and season to taste with salt.

PICO DE PIÑA

Chopped pineapple salsa

MAKES ABOUT 300G/10½OZ

½ pineapple, peeled, cored and chopped
1 white onion, chopped
1 habañero, deseeded and finely chopped
1 bunch coriander (cilantro), finely chopped
1 tbsp freshly squeezed lime juice
1 tbsp freshly squeezed orange juice
salt

1   Slightly sweet and great with grilled food. Mix everything together and season to taste.

Salsa verde.

Pico de pepino.

Salsa cruda.

Pico de gallo.

Salsa de aguacate.

Pico de piña.

Salsa de chipotle.

Curtidos.

Salsa de guajillo.

Cebolla morada.

Salsa de tomatitos.

Cebolla en vinagre.

SALSA DE CHIPOTLE

Smoky chilli sauce

MAKES ABOUT 300G/10½OZ

4 chipotle chillies
6 garlic cloves
150ml/5fl oz/scant ⅔ cup water
1 tsp apple cider vinegar
1 tsp salt

1   Roast the chilli and garlic in a dry, hot pan until coloured. Remove the stalks and seeds and soak the chillies in the water for 15 minutes. Blend everything to a salsa.

SALSA DE GUAJILLO

Hot chilli sauce

MAKES ABOUT 300G/10½OZ

10 dried guajillo chillies
1 thumb-size chunk of root ginger
2 garlic cloves
150ml/5fl oz/scant ⅔ cup water
1 tsp cider vinegar
salt

1   Boil the chillies, ginger and garlic in the water for 15 minutes. Remove the stalks and seeds from the chillies, then blend all the ingredients, strain and season to taste.

SALSA DE TOMATITOS

Cherry tomato salsa

MAKES ABOUT 550G/1LB 4OZ

500g/1lb 2oz cherry tomatoes, cut into chunks
1 white onion, cut into chunks
2 garlic cloves
2 jalapeño peppers
1 bunch coriander (cilantro)
1 tbsp freshly squeezed lime juice

1   Roast the tomatoes, onion, garlic and peppers on maximum heat in the oven until coloured. Cool. Blend with the coriander until smooth. Add the lime juice and season.

CURTIDOS

Pickled vegetables

MAKES A 450G/1LB JAR

1 carrot, sliced into coins
10 jalapeño peppers, deseeded
½ cauliflower, cut into florets
200ml/7fl oz/scant 1 cup distilled vinegar (12%)
200ml/7fl oz/scant 1 cup water
1 dried bay leaf
2 tsp salt
2 tsp granulated sugar

1   Put all the ingredients in a pan. Simmer over a low heat for 10 minutes. Cool, then chill.

CEBOLLA MORADA

Pickled red onion

MAKES 600G/1LB 5OZ

2 red onions
200ml/7fl oz/scant 1 cup cider vinegar
200ml/7fl oz/scant 1 cup freshly squeezed orange juice
200ml/7fl oz/scant 1 cup water
2 tsp salt
2 tsp granulated sugar

1   Slice the onion thinly. Mix the other ingredients together and pour over. Chill.

CEBOLLA EN VINAGRE

Pickled white onion

MAKES 500G/1LB 2OZ

2 white onions, finely sliced
1 jalapeño pepper, halved
200ml/7fl oz/scant 1 cup cider vinegar
1 dried bay leaf
200ml/7fl oz/scant 1 cup water
2 tsp salt
2 tsp granulated sugar

1   Put the onion and pepper in a bowl. Mix the other ingredients and pour over the top. Place in the refrigerator overnight.

GUACAMOLE
Mexican avocado salsa

Tostadas with
guacamole típico
and toasted
chapulines –
grasshoppers.

Guacamole comes in two main forms: chunky and smooth. The more coarsely chopped version works like a kind of avocado salad, as an accompaniment to tacos but also as a side dish to dip totopos (see page 52) or chicharrones (see page 52) into. If you're brave, flirt with the idea on the previous page and cover it with a layer of crisp chapulines and eat on a tostada (see page 16). The smoother variety is used exclusively as a salsa. It is quick, easy and goes perfectly with pretty much everything.

GUACAMOLE TÍPICO

Chunky guacamole

SERVES 4

2 jalapeño peppers, deseeded and chopped
1 bunch coriander (cilantro) leaves, chopped
½ white onion, chopped
4 avocados, peeled and pitted
2 tsp freshly squeezed lime juice (optional)
salt

1   Mexican guacamole contains little or no lime, so add it to taste. Mix the peppers, coriander (cilantro) and onion. Mash with a fork, then dice and add the avocado flesh. Stir gently but keep it chunky. Season to taste with salt and the lime juice.

GUACAMOLE TAQUERO

The taco chef's guacamole

SERVES 4

250g/9oz tomatillos or physalis
2 jalapeño peppers
½ white onion
2 garlic cloves
2 avocados, peeled and pitted
1 bunch coriander (cilantro)
1 tbsp freshly squeezed lime juice
salt

1   Preheat the oven to 200°C/400°F/gas 6. Cut the tomatillos and peppers in half and roast them with the peeled white onion and garlic until they have got a nice colour, about 20 minutes. Leave to cool. Blend with the other ingredients to a smooth salsa and season to taste with lime juice and a little salt.

MEXICAN INGREDIENTS
These sources offer international shipping but charges and additional duties may apply.
❈ **www.amazon.com / co.uk**: For tortilla presses, cal mexicana and other things.
❈ **www.casamexico.co.uk**: Mexican foods and other items. Online or Suffolk store.
❈ **www.coolchile.co.uk**: Online store with London-based outlet.
❈ **www.melburyandappleton**: Online store with East London warehouse.
❈ **www.mexgrocer.co.uk**: Online store.
❈ **www.shizzling.com**: Check out for a list of stores in London.
❈ **www.souschef.co.uk**: Online store.
❈ **www.spicetrekkers.com**: Online spices. Stores in Canada and France.

MEXICAN INGREDIENTS

Try to use these special ingredients for more
authentic flavours in your cooking.

Achiote (annatto) seeds and paste:
Give flavour and a lovely red colour.

Cal mexicana or
pickling lime: Slaked
lime for preparing
fresh masa.

Tajín seasoning and chamoy
sauce: Sweet-salt-spicy
toppings for fruit and
micheladas.

Dried hibiscus: Can be
found in tea shops.

Canela: Also known
as true cinnamon or
Ceylon cinnamon. You'll find
it in spice shops.

Piloncillo: Raw Mexican
sugar loaf.

Mexican chocolate: Often
available in delicatessens.

Crema.

Queso Oaxaca.

Queso fresco.

QUESOS Y CREMA

Homemade Mexican cheese and crema

Want to know how to give your tacos a stylish and super-authentic finish? You have to top them with the right kind of cheese. There are thousands of cheese varieties in Mexico, but I have focused on the three most important ones below: a crumbly cheese that doesn't melt at all, a stringy cheese with fantastic melting qualities, and a lovely thick cream to drizzle over the top. And the best thing of all: they are super easy to make (well, at least two of them are).

⁂ **Crema** The crema that is drizzled over some Mexican dishes tastes similar to crème fraîche, though it contains more fat and has a thinner consistency. Apart from adding creaminess to a dish, it balances the acidity and chilli heat in the food. Replace with: Even though it's super-easy to make your own crema (see overleaf), a good replacement is two parts of crème fraîche and one part single (light) cream. Mix together and drizzle attractively over the food using a spoon.

⁂ **Queso Oaxaca** This is a traditional cheese similar to mozzarella, made from long threads of cheese that are twirled together. When you unravel the cheese, long cheese strings are formed that are both pleasing to the eye and have just the right amount of fluffiness to go well with tostadas, tacos and antojitos or in quesadillas.

Replace with: Mozzarella. If you think it's boring to serve a lump of cheese on your tacos you can make your own cheat queso Oaxaca by heating a pan of water to 80°C/176°F. Dip a ball of mozzarella into the water to warm up, then stretch it out as far as your arms will reach, fold it in half and stretch out again. Continue until the cheese has turned into strings.

⁂ **Queso fresco** In addition to adding creaminess, a touch of acidity and pure dairy flavours, this fresh cheese doesn't melt, so looks beautiful crumbled over tacos, antojitos and grilled food.
Replace with: Difficult to replace as the flavour is like ricotta and the consistency is similar to feta, so it's best to make your own (see recipe overleaf). If you can't be bothered, replace with mild feta, a crumbly ricotta or the middle of a mild chèvre.

QUESO FRESCO

Fresh, crumbly non-melting cheese

MAKES 1 LARGE JAR

3 litres/105fl oz/13¼ cups full-fat milk
3 tbsp distilled vinegar (12%)
salt

1 This classic, crumbly topping is a must if you want a proper authentic look on your tacos and antojitos. So it's lucky that it's not much more difficult than making a cup of tea. And you can make a large batch and have cheese for weeks. Here's how to do it. Heat the milk to about 90°C/195°F, stirring gently. Remove from the heat, add the vinegar and leave to stand for 20–30 minutes. When the curd has separated from the whey, quickly cut a cross over the curd with a knife and place in a fine sieve or muslin. Save the whey and use as liquid for baking – or don't bother. Strain the curd over a bowl in the refrigerator for at least 2 hours or overnight. The cheese should be quite dry and deliciously crumbly. Season to taste with salt. Crumble over tacos. Take a bite. Smile.

CREMA

Creamy, runny crème fraîche

SERVES 4

500ml/17fl oz/generous 2 cups single (light) cream
1 tbsp crème fraîche

1 For a genuine Mexican crema, do this. Carefully heat the cream to 30°C/86°F in a pan. Whisk in the crème fraîche, pour the mixture into a jar with a loosely fitting lid and leave to stand at room temperature for about 12 hours. If it hasn't thickened, leave to stand for up to another 12 hours. When the crema is getting close to that perfectly creamy, runny consistency, transfer it to the refrigerator where it will thicken a little more. It will keep fresh in the refrigerator for up to 2 weeks.

QUESO OAXACA

Stringy cheese

SERVES 4

3 litres/105fl oz/13¼ cups full-fat milk
3 tbsp distilled vinegar (12%)
½ tsp rennet
3 limes
salt

1 For an authentic Mexican cheese, do this. Slowly heat the milk to 30°C/86°F. Whisk in the vinegar and the rennet, and slowly increase the heat to 32°C/90°F, 6–8 minutes. Remove the pan from the heat, cover with a lid and leave to stand for 1 hour. Cut a cross over the curd that forms then carefully heat to 42°C/108°F. Remove from the heat. Stir and leave to cool for 15 minutes. Strain through muslin but save the whey – you'll need it again soon.

2 Salt the whey as if it was pasta water and heat to about 80°C/176°F. Wearing a pair of new, thick rubber gloves, divide the curd into 3. Dip it into the hot whey and knead until it is shiny and soft. Stretch the cheese out as far as your arms can reach, fold in half and stretch it out again. Continue until you end up with a cheese made up of lots of strings. Place the strings on the table, sprinkle with salt and squeeze over some lime. Roll into a cheese ball. Store in a plastic bag in the refrigerator for up to 2 weeks.

MARIACHI 101
Cool songs to request from the mariachi band.

 ❀ **For the romantic:** Historia de un amor.
 ❀ **For the party animal**: El Borracho.
 ❀ **For the classic:** Carabina 30–30.
 ❀ **For the drinker**: El diaro de un borracho.
 ❀ **For the hard core**: La Martina.

LITTLE CHILLI SCHOOL
How to recognize your dried chillies.

Chipotle: Dried, smoked jalapeño with a distinctive smoky flavour and heat.

Guajillo: Mild with flavours of berries and green tea. Good for using in salsas.

Mulato: Dried poblano with flavours of coffee, cacao and dried fruit.

Pequín: Ancient chilli that grows wild. Crumble and sprinkle over food and fruit.

Pasilla de Oaxaca: Smoked version of the usual pasilla – used for mole negro.

Chilhuacle: Legendary chilli that's difficult to find. A must in genuine mole negro.

Cascabel: Beautiful, medium-hot chillies in the shape of and named after baby rattles.

ANTOJITOS

PART 2: TOSTADAS, QUESADILLAS AND OTHER SMALL DISHES

Gorditas made from blue corn.

GORDITAS Y TLACOYOS

Gorditas, tlacoyos and other kinds of antojitos

Although antojitos literally means 'little cravings', the term almost always refers to snacks made from ground nixtamalized corn. You see, tortillas are far from the only bread made from masa. There are literally hundreds of variations that, despite having the same base ingredient, taste different depending on their shape and how they are prepared. Try two of my favourites, gorditas and tlacoyos, or experiment with these variations.

Huaraches Oblong breads with a raised edge to hold in the salsa, these look like the sole of the sandals they are named after. Roll the masa to an oblong sausage and flatten to 5mm/¼in thick, using your fingers. Pinch all round to form an edge. Fry in a dry frying pan over a medium heat. Eat with salsa and your choice of topping.

Picados Round, small thick tortillas with a raised edge, like a little pizza. Roll the dough into small balls and flatten with your hands into a circle about 5mm/¼in thick. Pinch all round to form an edge. Fry in a dry frying pan over a medium heat. Eat with salsa and your choice of topping.

Empanadas Half-moon shaped masa breads with filling. Roll the dough into small balls, flatten in a tortilla press and add a filling of your choice (as long as it contains cheese). Fold in half, pinch the edges together and deep-fry until golden brown.

Garnachas Thick, deep-fried tortillas, made with equal amounts of masa and boiled, mashed sweet potato. Using your hands, flatten the mixture into a circle about 5mm/¼in thick. Pinch all round to form an edge. Deep-fry until golden brown and eat with salsa and a topping of your choice.

Sopes Thick tortillas with a high edge and crisp potato mixed into the masa. Mix equal amounts of masa and boiled, crumbled potatoes, leaving some larger bits. Using your hands, flatten the mixture into a circle about 5mm/¼in thick. Pinch all round to form an edge. Deep-fry until golden brown and crisp, and eat with salsa and your choice of topping.

Chalupitas Small tortillas dipped in salsa. Make corn tortillas as page 13. Dip into salsa verde or other salsa and deep-fry until crisp. Serve with more salsa, cheese and white onion.

GORDITAS

Small, thick corn breads with filling

MAKES 12

500g/1lb 2oz masa, fresh or made from Maseca (see page 13)
corn oil for deep-frying
salt

TO SERVE

filling of your choice from this book, such as frijoles refritos (see page 77), barbacoa (see page 80), carnitas (see page 66) or chorizo (see page 93)
shredded iceberg lettuce
queso fresco or crumbly goat's cheese (see page 30)
salsas of your choice (see pages 20–23)

1   Gorditas are small, fried corn breads that are soft on the inside, crisp on the outside and are opened up like a pitta bread. Everything that you can put into a taco you can put into a gordita. Here's how to do it. Divide the masa into 12 equal parts and roll into balls. Cover the dough with a piece of damp paper towel whenever you're not working it. Press the balls in a tortilla press (see page 13) until they are about 3–4mm/⅛–¼in thick, a bit thicker than a tortilla. In a pan heat the oil for deep-frying to 180–190˚C/350–375˚F. Quickly deep-fry your gorditas for 45 seconds until coloured and puffed up, turning once. Leave to drain on paper towels. Sprinkle with salt.

2   If your gorditas fail to puff up, you can eat them anyway, although they won't be as nice. Either the dough was too hard or you didn't use enough oil. The oil should cover the bread. Carefully cut open your gordita, stuff with the filling of your choice, shredded iceberg lettuce and plenty of queso fresco. Serve immediately with a couple of salsas.

TLACOYOS

Torpedo-shaped cheesy corn breads with bean filling

MAKES 8

500g/1lb 2oz masa, fresh or made from Maseca (see page 13)
200g/7oz/heaped ¾ cup frijoles refritos (see page 77)
queso Oaxaca or mozzarella (see page 30)
2 avocados
1 white onion
corn oil
salt

TO SERVE

salsas of your choice (see pages 20–23)

1   Tlacoyos are a speciality from Mexico City and can, depending on what kind of corn you use for the masa, be white, yellow or blue. They are often eaten with soup, as a bar snack or simply as a pick-me-up when you feel a bit down. If you can get hold of courgette (zucchini) flowers, use them raw for garnishing your tlacoyos. Very pretty! Divide the masa into 8 equal parts and roll into balls. Cover the dough with a piece of damp paper towel when you're not working it. Flatten the balls with the palm of your hand to about 1cm/½in thick. Add 1 tbsp frijoles refritos to each piece of dough and fold the dough over. Roll into a sausage and press; the tlacoyo should be about 1cm/½in thick.

2   Heat a frying pan over a low to medium heat and fry your tlacoyos until baked through, about 5 minutes on each side. Add a dash of oil to the pan, increase the heat a tad and fry one side until crisp. Turn over, add cheese and fry until the bottom is crisp too and the cheese has melted. Garnish with avocado slices and finely chopped white onion, and eat with some hot salsa and an ice-cold beer.

Tlacoyos.

Tostada de pulpo.

TOSTADAS

Fried corn tortillas with ceviche and other toppings

A 'cocteleria' is a stall where you buy ceviches, caldos and cocteles – different kinds of raw marinated fish, shellfish cocktails and soups. Often your ceviche is served on a tostada, which is a type of fried corn tortilla. The combination of the crisp tortilla and the hot, sour fish is fantastic, like the world's most luxurious crisps and dip. And it's very simple to make. Here are a few shellfish variations and one with slow-cooked ox cheek that is also delicious served in tacos.

TOSTADAS DE PULPO

Tostadas with grilled octopus

SERVES 4

500ml/17fl oz/generous 2 cups water
250ml/9fl oz/generous 1 cup white wine
250g/9oz octopus legs
1 dried bay leaf
1 tsp salt
3 garlic cloves
2 tbsp olive oil

TO SERVE

mayonesa de chipotle (see overleaf)
tostadas (see page 16)
pico de gallo (see page 20)
avocado

1   Bring the water and wine to the boil in a pan. Add the octopus and the bay leaf. Add salt. Lower the heat and simmer for about 1 hour until the octopus is nice and tender. Leave to cool in the liquid. Remove from the water and pull off the skin.

2   Light the grill. Cut the octopus into 1cm/½in chunks and thread them onto skewers. Grate the garlic into the oil and brush onto the octopus. Grill quickly. You can, of course, also grill the octopus on a griddle if you want. Spread mayonesa onto each tostada and top with octopus, pico de gallo and avocado.

TOSTADAS DE CEVICHE

Tostadas with finely chopped fish and prawns

SERVES 4

200g/7oz Atlantic halibut
200g/7oz raw fair trade prawns (shrimp)
1–2 limes
2 tomatoes
½ white onion
1 bunch coriander (cilantro)
salt

TO SERVE

mayonesa de chipotle (see overleaf)
tostadas (see page 16)
1 avocado
chilli sauce, such as Cholula

1   Finely chop the fish and the prawns (shrimp) until they are almost like mince, then squeeze the lime juice over the top. Leave in the refrigerator for 20 minutes, then drain off the lime juice or drink it. It's called leche de tigre in Peru and is supposed to be good for the immune system. Deseed and finely chop the tomatoes, onion and coriander (cilantro). Mix everything together and season with salt and more lime juice.

2   Spread mayonesa onto each tostada and top with the ceviche. Slice the avocado thinly, put on top and serve with chilli sauce.

TOSTADAS DE ATÚN

Tostadas with raw tuna

SERVES 4
1 leek
300g/10½oz tuna
3 tbsp Japanese soy sauce
3 tbsp freshly squeezed lime juice
oil for deep-frying
salt

TO SERVE
mayonesa de chipotle (see below)
tostadas (see page 16)
1 avocado

1   Cut the leek into thin julienne shreds. Heat
    the oil in a frying pan to about 180°C/350°F
    and deep-fry the leek in batches for about
    30 seconds until golden brown. Drain on
    paper towels. Sprinkle with salt.

MAYONESA DE CHIPOTLE

Chipotle mayonnaise

MAKES 200ML/7FL OZ/SCANT 1 CUP
1 tbsp freshly squeezed lime juice
1 large egg
½ tsp salt
150ml/5fl oz/scant ⅔ cup olive oil
1 dried chipotle chilli
2 garlic cloves

Blend the lime juice, egg and salt on a low
speed. Slowly pour in the oil until you have
a creamy mayonnaise. Toast the chilli and
garlic in a dry, hot frying pan until the chilli
puffs up and the garlic is soft. Discard stalk
and seeds and soak the chilli for 15 minutes.
Add to the mayonnaise with the garlic,
season with salt and blend till creamy.

2   Slice the tuna super thinly and marinate in
    the soy sauce and lime juice for 2 minutes.
    Drain. Spread mayonesa onto each tostada,
    top with tuna, thinly sliced avocado and
    finally a pile of deep-fried leek.

TOSTADAS DE CACHETE

Tostadas with slow-cooked ox cheek

SERVES 4
2 dried chipotle chillies
2 dried ancho chillies
8 garlic cloves
1 tbsp ancho chilli powder
2 tsp ground cumin
2 tsp dried coriander (cilantro)
2 tsp dried oregano
1kg/2lb 4oz ox cheek
330ml/11¼fl oz/scant 1½ cups light lager
oil for frying
salt and freshly ground black pepper

TO SERVE
tostadas (see page 16)
pico de gallo (see page 20)
queso fresco or crumbly goat's cheese (see page 30)
crema (see page 30)

1   Toast the chillies and garlic in a dry, hot
    frying pan until the chilli puffs up and the
    garlic has softened. Remove the stalks and
    seeds from the chilli and soak for 15 minutes.
    Blend to a smooth purée with the herbs and
    spices and some of the soaking liquid.

2   Preheat the oven to 90°C/195°F. Fry the ox
    cheeks in a little oil over a high heat. Sprinkle
    with salt and pepper. Transfer to a cast-iron
    lidded pot, pour over the purée and lager and
    cook in the oven for 6 hours. Pull the meat
    apart with forks and pour over sauce from
    the pot to make it juicy. Season to taste. Pile
    the meat onto a tostada and top with pico de
    gallo, queso fresco and a drizzle of crema.

From the top: Tostada de atún (here served with shredded iceberg lettuce instead of deep-fried leek), tostada de ceviche and tostada de cachete.

FLAUTAS

Deep-fried rolled corn tortillas with poached chicken

When you deep-fry corn tortillas they go crisp and beautifully golden in colour. That's why they're sometimes called 'dorados'; they both look and taste like gold. The absolute crispiest dorado is the flauta – the flute – a tightly rolled, filled corn tortilla. Flautas can be filled with most things – but the classic choice is some form of meat – because the combination of juicy meat and crunchy tortilla is a match made in heaven. Sometimes I eat two at a time. Don't be afraid to experiment with some of the other fillings in this book when making these.

1. Start by poaching the chicken. This is super-easy and surprisingly tasty as long as you don't overcook it. Remove the skin from the chicken fillets and place in a small saucepan. Cut the onion into wedges, crush the garlic, slice the lemon and place it all on top of the chicken fillets together with the bay leaf. Pour over enough water to barely cover the chicken. Salt the water and bring to the boil. Immediately lower the heat and leave the chicken to simmer gently for 10–12 minutes. Remove the chicken and leave to cool a little. You can prepare in advance up until this point if you want.

2. Use two forks to pull the chicken flesh apart. Mix with a couple of tablespoons of the salsa and save the rest for serving. Prepare the other accompaniments, too: finely shred the iceberg lettuce, crumble the cheese, prepare the crema, slice the lime and make extra salsa if you want.

3. Heat the oil in a frying pan to around 120°C/250°F. Dip the tortillas quickly in the oil so that they become soft and easier to roll. Remove from the pan then increase the heat to 180°C/350°F and start making your flautas. Add a little of the chicken mixture to each tortilla and roll into a cigar shape as tightly as you can. If you want long flautas as in the picture, overlap 2–3 tortillas and roll them carefully. Secure with a couple of cocktail sticks. Deep-fry two flautas at a time until golden and crisp. Turn over and do the same for the other side. Leave to drain on paper towels. Place two flautas on each plate, sprinkle with finely shredded iceberg lettuce, drizzle with the crema and sprinkle over some queso fresco. Serve with salsas of your choice and lime wedges.

SERVES 6

2 chicken fillets, 150g/5½oz each
1 onion
2 garlic cloves
1 lemon
1 dried bay leaf
1 batch salsa cruda (see page 20)
12 ready-made corn tortillas
oil for deep-frying
salt

TO SERVE

½ head iceberg lettuce
crema (see page 30)
queso fresco or crumbly goat's
　cheese (see page 30)
salsas of your choice (see pages
　20–23)
lime wedges

QUESADILLAS

Half-moon shaped filled tortillas

What we think of as a quesadilla – two wheat tortillas filled with cheese and ham and sliced into triangles – is called a 'sincronizada' in Mexico and is a kind of Latin American croque monsieur that's mostly served to tourists. In fact, a proper quesadilla doesn't have to contain cheese, and the word only really refers to a tortilla folded into a half-moon shape. That being said, we all love melted cheese, so it would seem remiss to skip it altogether, wouldn't it?

QUESADILLA CLÁSICO

Classic quesadilla

SERVES 4
queso Oaxaca or mozzarella (see page 30)
4 tortillas of your choice (see pages 13–16)
iceberg lettuce
filling of your choice (see below)
queso fresco or crumbly goat's cheese (see page 30)
salt

TO SERVE
salsa of your choice (see pages 20–23)

1 Grate the cheese over a tortilla and shred the iceberg lettuce finely. Have a little rummage in the refrigerator to find a suitable filling or keep it simple and just go with cheese. Season with a little salt. Fold the tortilla in half and fry in a dry frying pan on medium heat for about 2 minutes until the cheese has melted and the tortilla is crisp. Before serving, unfold the tortilla, add a spoonful of salsa and fold it again. Eat and be merry.

QUESADILLA DE CAMARÓN

Deep-fried quesadilla with prawns (shrimp)

SERVES 4
4 corn tortillas (see page 13)
1 boiled potato
100g/3½oz fresh prawns (shrimp)
queso Oaxaca or mozzarella (see page 30)
oil for deep-frying
salt

TO SERVE
salsa cruda (see page 20)
1 avocado

1 Heat the oil to 120°C/250°F. Dip each tortilla in the oil so that it is easier to fold. Increase the heat to 180°C/350°F. Mash the potato, finely chop the prawns (shrimp) and mix. Grate the cheese over the tortillas, add some prawn mix and fold. Secure with cocktail sticks and deep-fry for 3 minutes on each side. Drain on paper towels. Sprinkle with salt. Top with salsa and sliced avocado.

POPULAR QUESADILLA FILLINGS
❋ Courgette flowers ❋ Huitlacoche (Mexican corn truffle) ❋ Fried mushrooms ❋ Fried potatoes and chorizo (see page 93) ❋ Chicharrones (see page 52) ❋ Tinga (see page 74) ❋ Carnitas (see page 66)

Quesadillas made with blue corn tortillas.

TLAYUDAS
Charcoal-grilled corn dough pizzas

Some hungry customers eating freshly grilled tlayudas at the classic late-night food joint, Tlayudas Libres, in Oaxaca.

Horario
DE 9:00 P.M. a 4:00 A.M.

The street food joint Tlayudas Libres in Oaxaca opens at 9pm and doesn't close until it's time for those with more regular hours to go to work. They serve the classic Mexican late-night snack: tlayudas. Somewhere between a pizza and an enormous quesadilla, when you take your first bite you'll immediately understand why they're so popular. A chewy, crisp, smoky and slightly charred corn tortilla is folded over a filling of creamy beans, mild crema and loads of melted cheese.

1   A proper tlayuda is at least 36cm/14in in diameter, but how large you make yours depends on the size of your frying pan because before you grill the tlayuda, you have to pan-bake it. Here's how to do it. Divide the masa into 4 equal pieces (or more if you're making smaller tlayudas) and roll them into balls. Cover with damp paper towels. Take a clean plastic bag, preferably one that makes a rustling sound, and cut it so that you end up with two large pieces of plastic. Place a ball of masa in between them and flatten it out with your hands, rotating it at the same time until you have a 36cm/14in tortilla. Remove the top layer of plastic and place it dough-side down on a medium-hot, flat griddle pan or frying pan. Remove the other piece of plastic and pan-bake the tlayuda for about 2 minutes per side until it is baked through. Leave to dry a little.

2   Light a barbecue (grill) but don't use lighter fluid or charcoal briquettes. Grill the cecina, then remove the grill rack, because for maximum charcoal flavour, in Mexico you sometimes grill directly on the charcoal – so let's do it. Spread the fat on both sides of the tortilla. Top with beans, sliced avocado and lots of cheese and crema. Fold the tlayuda in half, then grill directly on the embers, about 3 minutes per side. You can also grill it in the normal way or on a griddle, but it doesn't taste the same. Serve immediately with a couple of grilled pieces of meat on top and a hot salsa on the side.

3   Alternatively, follow the instructions above, but leave the tlayuda open. Brush with the fat, spread with the beans, and add the cheese and the meat, as before, then drizzle with mole sauce. Grill directly on the embers, then top with sliced tomato, avocado as before, grilled pimiento and shredded romaine lettuce.

SERVES 6

500g/1lb 2oz masa, fresh or made from Maseca (see page 13)
cecina enchilada (see page 90)
100g/3½oz lard, shortening or butter
frijoles refritos (see page 77)
2 avocados
queso Oaxaca or mozzarella (see page 30)
crema (see page 30)
salsa of your choice (see pages 20–23)

Alternative version:
mole (see page 87)
tasajo (see page 90)
2 tomatoes
6 pimientos de padrón
romaine lettuce

*Classic, folded tlayuda
topped with grilled pork.
You'll find the open version
on the previous spread.*

The butcher in Frida Kahlo's hometown of Coyoacán proudly shows off his enormous chicharrones (pork rinds).

TACOS DE:
- SORTIDA
- CUERO
- NALIZA
- LENGUA
- COSTILLA

CHICHARRONES Y TOTOPOS
Deep-fried pork rinds, tortilla crisps and other snacks

In Mexican markets you will find enormous bits of pork rind, big as the whole side of a pig, that the customer breaks a piece from and pays for. Why the butchers make them so large I don't know, but they seem to take a lot of pride in keeping the rind as whole as possible when removing it and having a pan large enough to deep-fry it in. These chicharrones are a good way to use up more of the animal, plus they're ridiculously tasty. Just try dipping them in guacamole!

CHICHARRONES

Deep-fried pork rinds

MAKES 1 LARGE JAR
1 large piece of pork rind
1½ tsp salt
1 tsp granulated sugar
½ tsp ancho chilli powder
oil for deep-frying

1   Place the rind in a pan and cover with water. Boil for about 1½ hours until the rind is soft but doesn't break apart. Take it out carefully with a skimmer, then leave to cool in the refrigerator, placed flat and uncovered. After 2 hours, scrape off as much fat as you can. Put the rind on an oven rack with a baking tray underneath and cook in the oven on the lowest possible setting, something like 80°C/176–195°F. Bake the rind for about 8 hours until it's dry and hard. Break into pieces and store in a jar that you can take out as soon as you're peckish for some pig.

2   When it's time to eat, heat your deep-frying oil to about 190°C/375°F, chuck in a couple of rind pieces and watch how they magically expand and bubble up in front of your eyes. It takes about 15 seconds. Leave to drain on paper towels. Mix together the seasonings and sprinkle over. Eat as a snack with guacamole or as an accompaniment to tacos when you need that extra bit of crunch.

CACAHUATES

Hot home-roasted peanuts

MAKES ABOUT 375G/13OZ
275g/9¾oz/heaped 2 cups raw peanuts
100ml/3½fl oz/scant ½ cup freshly squeezed lime juice
1 tsp cayenne pepper
1 tsp ground paprika
1 tsp garlic powder
½ tsp salt

1   Preheat the oven to 100°C/210°F and roast the peanuts for 35–45 minutes, then turn off the oven. Stir in the lime juice and seasonings. Return to the cool oven and leave the nuts to dry for about 2 hours.

TOTOPOS

Homemade tortilla crisps

ready-made corn tortillas
oil for deep-frying
salt

1   Halve the tortillas (they'll be thinner and crispier than homemade). Heat 1cm/½in oil in a deep frying pan. Test a piece of tortilla and if it sizzles nicely, the oil is ready. Deep-fry the tortillas until crisp and golden, turning once. Drain on paper towels, then sprinkle with salt. Dip into salsa or guacamole. Not drinking a margarita with them is just wrong.

The most common snack in Oaxaca is neither pork rinds nor tortilla crisps, it's grasshoppers. Here, outside mercado 20 de noviembre, lots of different kinds of chapulines are on offer. They are pretty good actually. Especially served with a glass of mezcal. Or five.

TORTA AHOGADA

Meat sandwich swimming in chilli sauce

Torta ahogada means 'drowned sandwich' after the copious amounts of spicy salsa sauce in the dish. Traditional torta ahogadas come from the state of Jalisco and are served in a bolillo. A bolillo roll is white, easy to chew, and crisp – a bit like a baguette, which is an excellent alternative for the bolillo if you can't be bothered to bake. On a different note, Jalisco is where a lot of the things we associate with Mexico originate: mariachi music, tequila, sombreros and Mexican cowboys.

TORTA AHOGADA

Drowned sandwich

SERVES 6

600g/1lb 5oz carnitas (see page 66)
10 radishes
salsa of your choice (see pages 20–23)
cebolla morada (see page 23)
6 bolillos (see below) or 6 small crisp baguettes
3 avocados

1   Heat the carnitas – this dish is great for leftovers – slice the radishes, prepare the salsa and get out the cebolla morada. Toast the bolillos, remove some of the crumb if you like. then spread with the avocado. Add the meat and finish with radishes and cebolla morada or raw white onion if you're having one of those days. Serve with a jug of salsa on the side. Get sticky. Enjoy.

BOLILLOS

Crisp white bread

MAKES 8 BUNS

300g/10½oz/2½ cups strong white bread flour
10g/¼oz fresh yeast
2½ tbsp granulated sugar
1 tbsp salt, plus 1 tsp extra
150ml/5fl oz/scant ⅔ cup Mexican lager

Starter dough:
150g/5½oz/scant ¼ cup strong white bread flour
10g/¼oz fresh yeast
150ml/5fl oz/scant ⅔ cup Mexican lager

1   The day before you're baking the bread you have to make a starter dough. Do this by stirring together the flour, yeast and lager in a bowl. Cover with cling film (plastic wrap) and leave to rise overnight. The day after, mix the starter dough with the other ingredients and work in a dough mixer for about 10 minutes – about 20 minutes if you're using your hands. Leave to rise for about 2 hours until doubled in size.

2   Preheat the oven to 200°C/400°F/gas 6. Divide the dough into 6 equal pieces and roll them so that they look like American footballs – thicker in the middle and thinner towards the edges. Carefully flatten out a little. Cover with a dish towel and leave to rise for a further 40 minutes. Place on an oven tray and make a cut right across the buns with a sharp knife. Dissolve 1 tsp of salt in a little water, then brush it over the top. Place the buns on an oven rack over a water-filled tray in the oven and bake for 20–25 minutes until they're golden brown.

TORTA MILANESA

Sandwich with breaded chicken schnitzel

The Americans have their hamburgers, the Vietnamese their banh mi and the Swedes have their crispbread spread with butter. The absolutely most common Mexican sandwich, however, is torta Milanesa, a crisp bread filled with vegetables, cheese and a schnitzel made from flattened beef, pork or chicken. I prefer the latter version, even though all of them are pretty fantastic, of course.

TORTA MILANESA

Sandwich with breaded chicken schnitzel

SERVES 4
4 chicken fillets, about 100g/3½oz each
75g/2½oz/scant ⅔ cup plain (all-purpose) flour
2 eggs
30g/1oz/½ cup panko breadcrumbs
1 white onion
2 tomatoes
queso Oaxaca or mozzarella (see page 30)
4 pan telera buns (see recipe opposite)
1 avocado
mayonesa (see page 84)
oil for deep-frying
salt and freshly ground black pepper

1   Cut the chicken fillets half way through. Open them out and bash them to make four thin fillets. Salt and pepper generously. Turn them in the flour, then in the beaten egg, then in the panko. Heat the oil to about 180°C/350°F and deep-fry for 3 minutes on each side until the chicken is golden brown and cooked through. Leave to drain on paper towels.

2   Slice the white onion and the tomatoes thinly. Divide the cheese into thin strips using your hands. Halve the buns and 'spread' the bread with the avocado, add the freshly fried chicken schnitzel and top with onion, tomato, cheese and loads of mayonesa. Cut in half. Enjoy.

PAN TELERA

Classic simple white Mexican sandwich bread

MAKES 8 BUNS
10g/¼oz fresh yeast
400ml/14fl oz/1¾ cups tepid water
1 tbsp granulated sugar
1 tsp salt
500g/1lb 2oz/4 cups strong white bread flour
2 tbsp lard or butter

1   Dissolve the yeast in the water. Add the sugar, salt and flour and work in a dough mixer for about 4 minutes, or 8 minutes by hand, until you get a smooth dough. Add the fat in small dollops until everything is worked into the dough. Shape the dough into a ball, cover with cling film (plastic wrap) and leave to rise for 2 hours until doubled in size.

2   Preheat the oven to 200°C/400°F/gas 6. Divide the dough into 8 equal parts, roll them into oval balls and place on an oven tray. Flatten them out a bit with your hand, then press two deep tracks along the length of the bun using the handle of a wooden spoon (see image). Turn the buns over and do the same on the other side. Cover with a dish towel and leave to rise for 40 minutes. Press once more with the spoon handle in the same tracks, brush with water and bake in the middle of the oven for 15–20 minutes until golden brown. Leave to cool.

ELOTES Y ESQUITES

Grilled corn on the cob with queso fresco and corn salad with mayonnaise

Everywhere along the streets in Oaxaca you can find elotes and esquites, large, fresh corn on the cob that are either grilled and covered in mayo, chilli and queso fresco or cut up and served in plastic glasses that you eat from with a spoon. Often the corn is sold from beautifully decorated bicycles, so pretty that you want to cycle one all the way home. Instead you order another elote and make a promise to yourself that you will never eat corn in any other way than this.

ELOTES

Whole grilled corn on the cob with queso fresco

SERVES 4

4 fresh corn on the cob with husk
50g/1¾oz butter
½ lime
2 garlic cloves
100ml/3½fl oz/scant ½ cup ready-made
    mayonnaise
100ml/3½fl oz/scant ½ cup crema (see page 30)
ancho chilli powder
queso fresco (see page 30) or grated manchego
salt

1   Soak the corn for 10 minutes in its husk. Heat the grill, then grill the cobs in their husks until almost black, so the kernels are steamed inside and get a nice smoky flavour. Peel the corn and continue to grill on a high heat until they smell nice and the corn has a lovely roasted colour.

2   Melt the butter and brush over the corn. Sprinkle with salt. Squeeze the lime and garlic and mix with the mayo and crema. Skewer the corn and brush with the mayo.

3   Sprinkle with ancho chilli and then roll the cob into finely crumbled queso fresco or finely grated manchego. Queso fresco is more classic, plus it doesn't melt so will look nicer.

ESQUITES

Grilled or roasted corn salad with mayonnaise

SERVES 4

4 fresh corn on the cob
1 jalapeño pepper
½ bunch coriander (cilantro)
1 spring onion (scallion)
2 garlic cloves
2 tbsp ready-made mayonnaise
4 tbsp queso fresco (see page 30) or grated
    manchego
1 tbsp freshly squeezed lime juice
ancho chilli powder
vegetable oil
salt

1   If you have an outdoor grill, follow step 1 of the elotes recipe, then cut the corn kernels off the cob. If not, simply cut the kernels off the cob. Heat some oil in a frying pan and fry the corn until it's beautifully roasted. Sprinkle with salt.

2   Finely chop the pepper, coriander (cilantro) and spring onion (scallion). Grate the garlic and mix everything together with the mayonnaise, cheese and lime juice. Add the sweetcorn. Top with ancho chilli powder. Eat and enjoy.

TACOS

TACOS DE CARNITAS

Tacos with confit crispy pork

Carnitas is sometimes described as a Mexican version of pulled pork – but the truth is that the dish has more similarities with the French confit method, because the traditional way to cook carnitas is to leave large pieces of pork to slowly simmer away in enormous amounts of lard in large copper pots over an open fire. As a result of this, a good authentic carnita is recognized by the contrast between the tender, juicy confit meat and those crisp bits of pork that have almost deep fried. Yum. This homemade version is somewhat simplified and contains a little less fat, but just as much flavour.

1   Preheat the oven to 140°C/275°F/gas 1. Dice the pork into 3cm/1¼in cubes. Mix together the dry spices, salt and sugar and pat into the meat. Place the meat in a small ovenproof dish that is a snug fit. Squeeze the juice from 1 orange over the meat. Peel the garlic and put in between the meat chunks with the cinnamon stick, bay leaves and quartered onion. Add the lard. Slice the remaining un-peeled orange and arrange on top. Wrap the dish in foil and bake in the middle of the oven for 4 hours until the meat is tender.

2   Remove and discard the orange, onion, bay leaf and cinnamon stick. Strain the fatty cooking juices into a bowl and leave to cool while you deal with the meat. Take two forks and pull the pork collar into small pieces so that it gets nice and thread-like but still has a few chunks of meat. No one will be happy if it tastes like chewed toilet roll. Have a taste and add some extra salt, if needed. If you are serving up a taco dinner, you can prepare up until this point and place the meat and the cooking juices in the refrigerator until you're ready to eat.

3   It's crunch time! When it's time to eat, turn on the grill (broiler). Pour as much of the fatty juices as you think is decent over the pork and place in the oven. Leave it for about 10 minutes, take the dish out, stir it a little and return to the oven for a further 10 minutes. Serve immediately, together with the accompaniments listed to the right – and don't forget to stuff some chicharrones into your taco. They will give a wonderful crisp surprise.

SERVES 6

1.5kg/3lb 5oz pork collar or pork shoulder
1 tbsp smoked ground paprika
1 tbsp ancho chilli powder
1 tbsp salt
2 tbsp brown sugar
2 oranges
6 garlic cloves
5cm/1¾in Ceylon or standard cinnamon stick
2 dried bay leaves
1 onion
1oog/3½oz lard

TO SERVE

tortillas of your choice (see pages 13–16)
salsa verde (see page 20)
chicharrones (see page 52) or ready-made deep-fried pork rind
chopped coriander (cilantro) and white onion
lime wedges

A tacquero slices up
al pastor at the classic
El Huequito in Mexico City.

TACOS AL PASTOR

Tacos with homemade Mexican kebab and grilled pineapple

If Mexico City has a signature dish it's definitely tacos al pastor. The rotisserie method means that the outer layer of crispy pork is mixed with the softer layer within and, together with the deep chilli heat and a wedge of grilled pineapple, it is insanely good. One of those iconic street food dishes. The only question is, how do you recreate this at home? Turn the page to find out. But first some kebab history.

f you think that the spit of al pastor on the left looks like a kebab, that's because it is a kebab. You see, the dish was brought to Mexico by Lebanese immigrants in the 1930s. Tacos arabe, as the kebab was called, quickly gained popularity, and before long Mexican tacqueros started to experiment with the recipe. They swapped lamb for pork, added achiote and chilli, replaced the pitta bread with tortillas and, of course, placed a pineapple on top. And hey presto, the taco al pastor, or shepherd's tacos, was born.

Of course, the method of putting meat on a spit and grilling it over an open fire has probably been around for as long as humans who don't like to burn themselves have existed. Antique souvlaki skewers have been found in archaeological excavations, and grilling meat on horizontal, rotating rotisseries was common in Europe as early as the Middle Ages. But it wasn't until the end of the 19th century that the Turks thought of the idea that they could be used vertically as well. That way it was possible to add more meat, and as it cooked, the crisp outer layer could be cut off with a sharp knife. This so called doner kebab quickly spread across the Middle East, and from there to Mexico, and, during the 1960s, the Turkish gastarbeiters brought the kebab to Berlin – and from there out across the rest of Europe.

Today the kebab has travelled such a distance that one version has found its way back to the Middle East in the form of shawarma mexici – grilled chicken in Mexican adobo. This dish is not only really tasty but also works as a stark reminder of food's unrivalled ability to make the world just a little smaller and to bring its people together.

1   Start by making the adobo. Toast the dried chillies in a dry, medium-hot frying pan until they puff up and smell lovely. Remove the seeds and stalks and soak the chilli in pineapple juice and vinegar for 15 minutes. Blend with the rest of the adobo ingredients to a smooth paste. Slice the pork as thinly as possible against the meat fibres. Bash the slices out with a frying pan or similar so that they are really thin. Think schnitzel. Dip the meat into the adobo and layer with the bacon in a square ovenproof dish. Cover with cling film (plastic wrap). Marinate in the refrigerator for at least 3 hours.

2   Preheat the oven to 200°C/400°F/gas 6. Roast the meat in the middle of the oven for about 3 hours. Leave to cool, then chuck the whole thing into the refrigerator for a couple of hours, preferably a whole day. This is to allow the fat to set so that it's easier to slice thinly. You can prepare up until this point for a dinner party or other occasion.

3   When dinner time is approaching, preheat the oven to 200°C/400°F/gas 6. Peel then slice the pineapple into 4 wedges, remove the core and roast the pieces for 20 minutes. Turn the brick-shaped piece of set meat out onto a chopping board. Slice the meat very thinly, then fry in a frying pan over a high heat until crisp, using the fat as well. Season to taste with salt. Serve in a tortilla together with thinly sliced pineapple, salsa, chopped coriander (cilantro) and white onion.

SERVES 6

1–1.5kg/2lb 4oz–3lb 5oz pork collar, preferably high fat
140g/5oz bacon
1 pineapple
salt

Adobo:
2 dried guajillo chillies
2 dried ancho chillies
200ml/7fl oz/scant 1 cup pineapple juice
2 tbsp distilled vinegar (12%)
50g/1¾oz achiote paste
1 chicken stock cube
1 whole garlic bulb
1 tsp ground cumin
3cm/1¼in Ceylon or standard cinnamon stick
1 tbsp salt

TO SERVE
tortillas (see pages 13–16)
salsa verde (see page 20)
chopped coriander (cilantro) and white onion
lime wedges

MEXICO CITY'S BEST
TACOS AL PASTOR

EL HUEQUITO The 'little hole in the wall' has served up sublime tacos al pastor at the same address since 1959. *Address: Ayuntamiento 21, El Centro. www.elhuequito.com.mx*

EL TIZONCITO This restaurant claims to have invented the dish, even though divided opinions are likely to exist in this regard. It's so popular that nowadays it's a chain. *Address: Tamaulipas 122, La Condesa. www.eltizoncito.com.mx*

EL FAROLITO You'll find this much-loved place just across the road from the equally famous El Califa (www.elcalifa.com.mx) in the chic neighbourhood of La Condesa. Opened in 1966. *Address: Altata 19 Hipódromo, La Condesa. www.taqueriaselfarolito.com.mx*

TACOS DE GUISADOS
Tacos with four different kinds of stew

Below: Tacos with frijoles refritos and tinga de pollo. In one of the pots pictured on the left you can also spot the vegetarian guisado, acelgas con papas.

Mexican fast food isn't particularly fast. In fact, it has more in common with the slow-food movement. This is because most things are made from scratch in the kitchen at home, then packed onto a bike and transported to the street kitchen where they're served to voraciously snacking customers. This is especially true of the guisados – comfort food for taco lovers – wonderfully warming stews wrapped in a fresh tortilla with rice and topped with cheese and salsa.

TINGA DE POLLO
Chicken in chipotle sauce

SERVES 6

3 dried chipotle chillies
3 garlic cloves
400g/14oz canned plum tomatoes
½ white onion
1 tsp dried oregano
1 tsp ground cumin
1 tsp granulated sugar
700g/1lb 9oz chicken thighs on the bone
1 dried bay leaf
corn oil for frying
salt and freshly ground black pepper

TO SERVE

tortillas of your choice (see pages 13–16)
salsas of your choice (see pages 20–23)
curtidos (see page 23)
cooked long-grain rice

1   Toast the chillies and garlic in a hot dry frying pan until the chillies puff up and the garlic has started to soften. Remove the stalks and seeds from the chillies and soak for 15 minutes. Blend the chillies and garlic with the tomatoes, onion, oregano, ground cumin and sugar. Fry the chicken thighs, skin-side down, in oil until the skin is crisp, then turn over. Sprinkle with salt and pepper. Pour the tomato sauce over the top, but not so much that the skin side gets soggy. Add the bay leaf. Leave to simmer gently for 30 minutes. Season to taste with salt and pepper. Serve by placing the whole frying pan on the table, together with the accompaniments, and let everyone pull their own bit of meat off the chicken bones, crunch on the skin and help themselves to the chilli sauce.

ACELGAS CON PAPAS
Leafy greens and potatoes

SERVES 4

4 potatoes
2 onions
3 garlic cloves
1 tbsp dried chilli (hot pepper) flakes
1 large bunch of chard, kale or cavolo nero
200ml/7fl oz/scant 1 cup chicken or vegetable stock
olive oil for frying
salt and freshly ground black pepper

TO SERVE

tortillas of your choice (see pages 13–16)
salsas of your choice (see pages 20–23)
queso fresco or crumbly goat's cheese (see page 30)

1   Acelgas means chard, but this vegetarian guisado can be made from pretty much any leafy greens. Preheat the oven to 225°C/450°F/gas 8. Cut the potato into 2cm/¾in cubes, stir in some oil and roast for 45 minutes until golden brown and crisp.

Life enjoyment of the highest kind outside the guisado joint, Tacos Hola!, in Mexico City's La Condesa.

Picadillo

Slice the onion thinly and fry in some oil in a frying pan over a medium heat until caramelized. Season to taste with salt. Slice the garlic and add with the chilli and leafy greens, coarsely chopped and stalks removed. Add salt, pepper and stock and boil for 10 minutes until the liquid has nearly evaporated. Just before serving, mix together the greens and potatoes.

FRIJOLES REFRITOS
Creamy refried beans

SERVES 4
250g/9oz dried black beans
1 tbsp dried epazote or half oregano and half dried dill
3 garlic cloves
1 white onion
6 tbsp olive oil or lard
salt and freshly ground black pepper

TO SERVE
tortillas of your choice (see pages 13–16)
salsas of your choice (see pages 20–23)
queso fresco or crumbly goat's cheese (see page 30)
cooked long-grain rice

1   Soak the beans well covered in water for 8–10 hours. Drain and add the beans to a pan with the epazote, 2 garlic cloves and ½ white onion. Cover the beans by 5cm/1¾in with fresh water. Bring to the boil, lower the heat and simmer gently for about 1 hour until the beans are soft. Drain off the water but save it for now. Throw away the garlic and onion.

2   Heat the fat in a frying pan over a medium heat. Finely chop the remaining onion and garlic clove and fry until transparent. Add the beans and fry for a bit longer. Add 200ml/7fl oz/scant 1 cup of the saved cooking water, then mash the beans using a potato masher or a hand-held blender for a creamier result. You can also leave some beans whole. Season with salt and pepper. Cook the beans

a little more if they are too watery. If too thick, add more cooking water. Serve with almost any taco in the book.

PICADILLO
Weekday chuck steak stew

SERVES 8
2 onions
4 garlic cloves
250g/9oz uncooked chorizo
1kg/2lb 4oz beef chuck steak
400g/14oz canned plum tomatoes
1 tbsp granulated sugar
1 tbsp chilli powder
2 tsp ground cumin
½ tsp ground Ceylon or standard cinnamon
2 dried bay leaves
oil for frying
salt and freshly ground black pepper

Adobo:
6 dried ancho chillies
3 tbsp red wine vinegar

TO SERVE
tortillas of your choice (see pages 13–16)
salsas of your choice (see pages 20–23)

1   Finely chop the onions and garlic and fry with the chorizo in a little oil in a cast-iron pan over a medium heat for a few minutes. Take out of the pan. Cut the chuck into cubes and fry in batches until coloured. Add the onion, garlic, chorizo, tomatoes, sugar and spices. Sprinkle with salt and pepper.

2   Make the adobo. Toast the chillies until they puff up and smell nice. Remove the stalks and seeds and soak for 15 minutes until soft. Mix with a little soaking water and the vinegar and blend to a smooth purée. Pour over the meat. Simmer gently, covered, for at least 4 hours until the meat has softened. Serve with tortillas and salsas.

BARBACOA DE OAXACA
Slow-cooked lamb steak with vegetable soup

The pitmaster at the restaurant La Capilla in the village of Zaachila signals that the food is ready. The barbacoa is prepared the day before by firing in a pit for several hours. A freshly slaughtered goat is buried together with vegetables and a bottle of mezcal. A crucifix is placed in the ground. The morning after, the warm mezcal is served together with the tender meat and the soup.

...hough traditional barbacoa is made from a freshly slaughtered goat .... in a pit in the ground, I've made it easier for you, your lawn and your neighbours by suggesting a ready-prepared lamb steak that is cooked in the oven. The wonderful caldo, or soup, that comes out of the vegetables and the frying juices can be served as a separate starter or together with your tacos.

1. Soak the beans in water for a day before your meal. If you forget, you can use canned beans but they are not quite as good. Salt the lamb steak and fry in a little oil in a hot ovenproof pan until browned. Add some more salt and a generous amount of pepper. Start making the adobo. Roast the dried chillies in a dry medium-hot pan until they puff up and the kitchen smells nice. Discard the seeds and stalks and soak the chillies in water and vinegar for 15 minutes. Add the remaining adobo ingredients and blend to a smooth paste.

2. Preheat the oven to 120°C/250°F/gas ½. Sort out the vegetables: neatly dice the potato, carrot and celery and finely chop the onion. Transfer to an ovenproof pan with a lid and add the beans and epazote if you can get hold of it. Rub the lamb steak with the adobo and place the meat on top of the vegetables. The meat should be braised, or cooked slowly with a bit of liquid so fill the pan with water so that the meat is covered by one-third. Cover with the lid and place in the middle of the oven for 4–5 hours. The meat should fall apart nicely without being dry, which normally means an inside temperature of around 87°C/190°F.

3. Cut the corn tortillas into thin strips and deep-fry in oil until crisp. Dice the avocados, finely slice the peppers and cut the lime into wedges. Chop the coriander (cilantro) and white onion and mix together. Put the tortillas and salsa on the table. Take the meat out of the pan. Skim off the fat and season the rest with salt and pepper. Put the meat and soup on the table. Pour out a large, traditional mezcal for everyone and explain which accompaniments are for the soup and which are for the tacos. Also, encourage people not to dip the tacos in the soup and, of course, to help themselves to some extra mezcal.

SERVES 6
2kg/4lb 8oz lamb steak on the bone
170g/6oz/1 cup dried pinto beans
3 large firm potatoes
2 carrots
3 celery stalks
1 white onion
1 tbsp dried epazote
oil for deep-frying and cooking
salt and ground black pepper

Adobo:
2 dried guajillo chillies
2 dried ancho chillies
200ml/7fl oz/scant 1 cup water
2 tbsp distilled vinegar (12%)
1 whole garlic bulb
1 tbsp ground cumin
1 tsp ground coriander seeds
1 tbsp salt
1 tbsp granulated sugar

Soup accompaniments:
6–8 ready-made corn tortillas
2 avocados
6 jalapeño peppers
3 limes

TO SERVE
tortillas (see pages 13–16)
salsas of your choice (see pages 20–23)
chopped coriander (cilantro) and white onion

TACOS DE LENGUA

Tacos with slow-cooked fried beef tongue

I don't want to frighten anyone with this, but in other countries they are less sensitive about eating the whole animal than in the plastic-wrapped, fillet-loving, squeamish Western world. And why not? Because what does it say about us, that we're put off when we see pig's trotters or sheep testicles, but think nothing about eating four cheap sausages in one go as part of our dinner? In less wealthy countries they can't afford the luxury of blind pickiness, and in the fast food stalls of Mexico it's not uncommon to find tacos containing, for example, eyes, brain or even uterus. But before we take our taco interest to its logical end point, I think we should warm up slowly with a tongue taco.

1   Peel and coarsely chop the onions, carrots, celery and garlic and add to a pan with the tongue. Add the peppercorns, bay leaves and salt. Add water so it just covers the ingredients. Bring to the boil, skim off the foam, then lower the heat. Simmer for about 3 hours until the meat is tender. Remove the pan from the heat and leave the tongue to cool in the liquid.

2   Now it's time for the potentially disgusting part. You don't want to eat that rough upper part of the tongue that brings on thoughts of parent-free house parties rather than of festive dinners with friends, so you need to peel the tongue. You do this simply by pulling off the skin in large strips with your fingers. If it's stuck, you can use a knife. Give the skin to the dog, then cut the tongue into small cubes. You can prepare in advance up until this point.

3   When it's time to eat, heat a little oil in a frying pan and fry the tongue until crisp. Serve in a warm tortilla with your chosen salsa and feel how the tongue melts on your tongue.

SERVES 6
2 onions
2 carrots
2 celery stalks
1 whole garlic bulb
1 beef tongue, about 1kg/2lb 4oz
1 tbsp whole black peppercorns
6 dried bay leaves
2 tbsp salt
oil

TO SERVE
tortillas of your choice (see
    pages 13–16)
pico de gallo (see page 20)
guacamole (see page 26)

GLOSSARY FOR ADVENTUROUS TACO LOVERS

⊗ Buche: Pig's oesophagus   ⊗ Cabeza: Cow's head   ⊗ Labios: Cow's lips   ⊗ Ojos: Eyes, most often from sheep   ⊗ Orejas: Pig's or cow's ears   ⊗ Sesos: Cow's brain   ⊗ Tripa: Stomach.

TACOS DE PESCADO

Tacos with deep-fried fish and cabbage salad

Quick, tasty, healthy and simple. Crisp, crunchy, sour, hot, salty and smooth. It's easy to see why fish tacos have started to become a weekday classic around the world. I eat this myself once a week. If you're the same and want some variation, you can replace the fish with pretty much any (edible) sea creature: prawns (shrimp), squid or oysters. Vegetarians can deep-fry vegetables like cauliflower, mushrooms, sweet potato or even avocado – that's pretty amazing too.

1   For this dish you'll want the fish to be as freshly fried and crisp as possible, so prepare everything else in advance: tortillas, pico de gallo and other accompaniments. The cabbage salad is the simplest possible. Just slice the cabbage as thinly as you can, place the shreds in a sieve, sprinkle with salt and leave to soften while you cook the rest of the food. The mayonesa isn't difficult either. Just press the garlic and mix together with the other ingredients. Add chilli sauce and salt to taste.

2   It's deep-frying time! Cut the fish into pieces about 6–8cm/2½–3¼in long and 2–3cm/¾–1¼in thick – they should look almost like a long, thick thumb. Sprinkle with salt and thread onto skewers. That way they are less sticky, they don't get stuck to the bottom of the fryer and you can move them around in the oil so that the batter gets speed lines and maximum crispiness is achieved. For the batter, mix together the flours in a bowl. Heat the oil to 180°C/350°F, and once you've done that, whisk the egg yolk, tequila and ice-cold sparkling water into your flour mixture. Holding onto the skewer, dip the fish into the batter. Add to the oil and move the fish around for a couple of seconds. The alcohol evaporates straight away and contributes to the crispiness, so this dish is fully child proof. Deep-fry for a couple of minutes. When the batter has turned lightly golden, take out the fish and leave to drain on paper towels. Sprinkle with salt.

3   Assemble the taco by placing a piece of deep-fried fish in the tortilla and removing the skewer. Top with the cabbage salad, pico de gallo and cebolla morada, and finally drizzle over lots of mayonesa. Serve with lime wedges, some extra chilli sauce and an ice-cold beer.

SERVES 4

500g/1lb 2oz fish of your choice, such as cod
¼ red or white cabbage
salt

Deep-frying batter:
75g/2½oz/scant ⅔ cup rice flour
75g/2½oz/scant ⅔ cup plain (all-purpose) flour
1 egg yolk
3 tbsp tequila
150ml/5fl oz/scant ⅔ cup ice-cold sparkling water
oil for deep-frying

Mayonesa:
4 garlic cloves
1 freshly squeezed lime
100ml/3½fl oz/scant ½ cup ready-made mayonnaise
100ml/3½fl oz/scant ½ cup crema (see page 30)
chilli sauce, such as Cholula

TO SERVE
tortillas (see pages 13–16)
pico de gallo (see page 20)
cebolla morado (see page 23)
chilli sauce, such as Cholula
lime wedges

POLLO CON MOLE NEGRO

Tacos with chicken, rice and black mole sauce

Out of the seven world-famous mole sauces, it's the mole negro, the black mole with chocolate, that is the undisputed ruler. This is proper feast food. The mole negro, you see, is spicy, aromatic, and complex and when it's well balanced it is truly one of the world's great meals. This recipe is based on the mole that the chef Rick Bayliss made for President Obama in the White House.

1 Start with the mole. Remove the stalks and seeds from the chillies. If you can find smoked pasilla Oaxaca or chilhuacle, use them instead of the chipotle and ancho – although a mole nerd orders the correct chillies online – because this is one dish that deserves the same ardent fan base as chilli and hamburgers. Heat the oil and deep-fry the dried chillies for 30 seconds, remove, then soak in water for 30 minutes.

2 Roast the white onion and garlic in a dry frying pan until they are soft and have turned a nice colour. Toast two slices of bread in a toaster on a high setting, then blend with the onion, garlic, cloves, cinnamon, thyme, oregano, banana, a pinch of black pepper and 500ml/17fl oz/generous 2 cups of the stock into a fine purée. Set aside. Toast the sesame seeds, pecan nuts, peanuts and almonds in a dry frying pan until nicely coloured. Blend to a smooth purée with a further 500ml/17fl oz/generous 2 cups of the stock. No need to wash the blender in between. Set aside. Blend the tomatoes and tomatillos with a further 500ml/17fl oz/generous 2 cups of the stock and set aside in a third bowl. Finally, blend the soaked chilli with the remaining 500ml/17fl oz/generous 2 cups of stock.

3 Heat 3 tbsp of the chilli frying oil in a large pan over a medium heat. Add the tomato purée and boil for 20 minutes, stirring. Add the nut purée and boil for 10 minutes. Do the same with the banana purée, then the chilli purée, then boil for 30 minutes until reduced and thickened. Grate in the chocolate, add the sugar, cover, lower the heat and simmer gently for 1 hour. Check the seasoning. Cut the chickens into four thighs and four fillets. Add the thighs to the mole and cook for 15 minutes, then add the fillets and cook for 25 minutes. Serve with rice, tortillas and lime wedges. You can freeze any leftover mole and serve as salsa.

SERVES 8

1 dried mulato chilli
6 dried chilhuacle chillies
6 dried pasilla Oaxaca
1 dried chipotle chilli
½ white onion
4 garlic cloves
2 slices white bread
1 pinch ground cloves
1 pinch ground Ceylon or
   standard cinnamon
1 pinch dried thyme
1 tsp dried oregano
½ ripe banana
2 litres/3½ pints/8 cups chicken
   stock
50g/1¾oz/⅓ cup sesame seeds
25g/1oz/scant ½ cup each
   unsalted pecan nuts, peanuts
   and almonds
6 plum tomatoes
2 tomatillos or 8 physalis
50g/1¾oz/heaped ⅓ cup grated
   Mexican chocolate
3 tbsp granulated sugar
2 chickens, about 1.3kg/3lb each
oil for deep-frying
salt and ground black pepper

TO SERVE

cooked long-grain rice, tortillas
   (see pages 13–16) and lime
   wedges

CARNES ASADAS
Tacos with grilled, thinly sliced meat and vegetables

High heat and thinly sliced, tough but flavourful meat equals maximum amount of grill flavour. The spring onions (scallions) and chillies are cooked directly on the embers.

If I was only allowed to cook one recipe from this book, it would be this, because it offers maximum flavour for minimum effort. All you have to do is to grill meat, chop vegetables, bake tortilla and then run round the garden and flip out. Choose one of the meat options and a couple of accompaniments for a great weekday dinner. Grill all three meats and prepare all the accompaniments for a feast that is second to none. Grilled onion and chilli is, however, always a must.

CECINA ENCHILADA
Charcoal-grilled, chilli marinated pork

SERVES 4
1kg/2lb 4oz whole boneless pork loin, or a whole
   pork collar

Adobo:
10 dried guajillo chilies
150ml/5fl oz/scant ⅔ cup water
4 garlic cloves
2 tsp cider vinegar
3 tsp salt
1 tsp granulated sugar
½ tsp ground cumin
½ tsp freshly ground black pepper
3cm/1¼in Ceylon or standard cinnamon stick

1   Slice the meat according to the instructions on page 93, then start the adobo. Toast the chillies in a hot dry frying pan until they puff up and smell nice. Remove the stalks and seeds and leave to soak in water for 15 minutes. Put the chillies in a blender, add the water and the other ingredients and blend to a smooth sauce. Spread evenly over the accordion-sliced meat, then fold the meat again. Marinate in the refrigerator for at least 2 hours.

2   Light your grill and make it as hot as possible. Grill the meat quickly, just a few minutes on each side. Cut into strips against

the grain of the fibres and serve in a tortilla with a few of the accompaniments. Cowards can even make this on a griddle on the stove.

TASAJO
Charcoal-grilled accordion-sliced beef

SERVES 4
1kg/2lb 4oz whole flank steak or skirt steak
salt and freshly ground black pepper

1   Prepare the meat as on page 93. Flank steak and skirt lend themselves perfectly to this method, as they are tough but flavourful cuts. Light your grill and make it as hot as possible. Grill the thinly sliced meat quickly, just a few minutes on each side. Season, then leave to rest for a minute before cutting into

GRILL ACCOMPANIMENTS
• Grilled pimientos de padrón
• Grilled salad onion
• Tortillas of your choice (see pages 13–16)
• Pico de gallo (see page 20)
• Salsa de aguacate (see page 20)
• Chopped coriander (cilantro) and onion
• Sliced peeled cucumber
• Sliced radishes
• Lime wedges
• Chilli sauce

Grilled, accordion-sliced
flank steak – tasajo – with
corn tortillas, grilled onion
and chilli.

Grilled chilli-marinated pork, cecina enchilada, with accompaniments.

strips against the grain. Serve in a tortilla with your choice of accompaniments. It can also be prepared on a griddle on the stove.

CHORIZO

Charcoal-grilled homemade sausage

SERVES 4

4 dried ancho chillies
2 tbsp finely chopped garlic
½ tsp ground Ceylon or standard cinnamon
½ tsp freshly ground white pepper
1 tsp dried oregano
1 tsp dried coriander (cilantro)
1 tsp ancho chilli powder
2 tbsp smoked ground paprika
4 tsp salt
6 tbsp cider vinegar
1 lager
2kg/4lb 8oz pork shoulder
sausage casing

1   Toast the chillies in a hot dry frying pan until they puff up and smell nice. Remove the stalks and seeds, then soak the chillies in water for 30 minutes. Blend with some of the soaking water to a smooth paste. Mix the paste with the rest of the ingredients (except the pork and sausage casing) in a large bowl. Cut the pork into cubes small enough to fit into the mincer and mix with the paste. Freeze for 1 hour.

2   Mince the meat using the finest blade. Stir and transfer to the refrigerator immediately. Thoroughly rinse the sausage casing, attach the sausage stuffing nozzle to the mincer, slip the whole casing onto the nozzle and tie a knot at the end. Carefully press the chilled sausage meat into the casing as a single long sausage. Then form short, fat sausages by tying a knot with a piece of kitchen string about every 5cm/1¾in.

3   Grill the sausages and serve in tortillas with your choice of accompaniments from page 90. If you prefer, you can griddle them on the hob (stovetop). Any leftover sausages may be frozen. You can also skip stuffing the sausage meat into the casing and instead fry it in patties as you might do with mince. They make awesome breakfast tacos with salsa, fried grated potato, tortillas and fried eggs.

HOW TO ACCORDION-SLICE YOUR MEAT

Place your chunk of meat so that the meat fibres are lying diagonally towards you. Place a firm hand on top and then cut with a super-sharp knife parallel to the chopping board as close as you possibly can. Don't cut all the way through the meat, but stop when you're about 2cm/¾in from the edge. Pull out the knife then slice the meat a little bit above the first cut, but in the opposite direction. Continue until the whole chunk of meat is cut up so that you can unfold it into a single long slice, a bit like a meat accordion. During transport and marinating you can keep it folded up. Unfold it when you want to show off your knife skills. When you grill the meat, just cut off suitably sized pieces and chuck them onto the grill rack.

In the carnes asadas hall at mercado de 20 de noviembre in Oaxaca you can get the meal of your lifetime in an incredible setting – and all for only a couple of pounds.

DULCES

PART 4: CHURROS, PALETAS AND OTHER SWEET THINGS

FRUTA CRISTALIZADA
Mexican candied fruit

In many Mexican towns you can find beautiful art deco sweet shops filled with amazing artisan sweets. Fruta cristalizada is the star – fruit boiled in sugar until it has almost turned transparent – tasting as good as a jelly sweet and as beautiful as a stained glass window. They can be eaten as they are or can be chopped and sprinkled over your porridge, yoghurt, pancakes, cakes or ice cream.

FRUTA CRISTALIZADA

Candied fruit

MAKES 1.5KG/3LB 5OZ

1kg/2lb 4oz fruit, such as pineapple, papaya, plum, pear or fig, washed
2 litres/70fl oz/8 cups water
750g/1lb 10oz/heaped 4 cups granulated sugar

1   Cut large fruit into smaller pieces; smaller fruits are prettiest left as they are. Prick the fruit with a fork and place in a large pan, cover with the water and add the sugar. Simmer for 1 hour, without bringing it to the boil, and then leave to cool overnight in the sugar syrup. Repeat this for a further 2 days.

2   On the fourth day, take out the fruit and place it on a rack over a deep oven dish. Reduce the sugar syrup until thick and golden yellow, about 30 minutes over a low heat, and pour it over the top so the fruit shines. Heat the oven to its lowest setting (50°C/122°F), then dry the fruit for 8–12 hours with the oven door ajar. Store in a cool, dry place for up to a year.

LIMONES RELLENOS

Coconut-filled limes

MAKES 12 SWEETS

6 small limes
200ml/7fl oz/scant 1 cup water
150g/5½oz/heaped ¾ cup granulated sugar
a few drops of green food colouring

Filling:
60g/2¼oz/heaped ¾ cup grated coconut
4 tbsp sweetened condensed milk
1 tbsp freshly squeezed lime juice
1 pinch salt

1   These beautiful little sweets were Frida Kahlo's favourites, and therefore they are also my favourites. Here's how to make them. Halve the limes and remove the flesh. Place both in a pan and cover with water. Bring to the boil, lower the heat and simmer for 20 minutes. Strain off the water and repeat three times to get rid of the bitterness in the peel. If you want to make fruta cristalizada from lime or lemon peel this is how to prepare them. Leave to cool and scrape off the white pith from the inside with a teaspoon. Put the measured water, the sugar, food colouring and peel in a pan and bring to the boil. Simmer gently over a fairly low heat until the sugar water has turned into a thick syrup, about 45 minutes. Remove from the heat and leave to cool completely.

2   Preheat the oven to its lowest setting (50°C/122°F), then dry the lime peel for about 2 hours with the oven door ajar. Just before they are dry, get started on the filling. Stir together the coconut, condensed milk, lime juice and salt. Super simple! Then fill each peel with coconut filling and put two together so that they look like whole limes. Or if you want slightly smaller sweets, only scoop up the filling into half a peel. It's up to you.

PALETAS

Handmade ice lollies with natural ingredients

The Mexicans are the best in the world when it comes to ice lollies. Even if they are sometimes a bit overzealous with the food colouring, the ice lollies are always handmade and contain fresh fruit and natural ingredients – not an artificial flavour enhancer in sight. Mexican paletas are often quite chunky, so don't be afraid of adding nuts, biscuit crumbs and fruit chunks to the ice.

PALETAS DE LIMÓN

Lime ice lollies

MAKES 6–8 ICE LOLLIES
6 limes
1 litre/35fl oz/4⅓ cups water
190g/6¾oz/1 cup granulated sugar

1   Don't be fooled by the simplicity of this recipe; this is the tastiest ice lolly in the world. And that's that. Zest the limes and steep the peel in the water for 1 hour. Pour the zest water into a pan, add the sugar, bring to the boil and simmer gently for 20 minutes. Take off the heat and add the juice of 3 limes. Cool, then leave in the refrigerator for 4 hours. Strain off the zest, pour into paleta moulds and freeze for 2 hours. Add the lolly sticks and freeze for at least 4 hours more.

PALETAS DE CAJETA

Goat caramel ice cream

MAKES 6–8 ICE LOLLIES
300ml/10½fl oz/1¼ cups single (light) cream
150ml/5fl oz/scant ⅔ cup goat's or cow's milk
40g/1½oz/¼ cup granulated sugar
1 vanilla pod
3 egg yolks
100ml/3½fl oz/scant ½ cup cajeta (see page 110)

1   Bring the cream, milk and sugar to the boil in a pan. Scrape out the vanilla pod and add the seeds and the pod. Whisk the egg yolks in a separate bowl. Whisk half of the cream mixture into the yolks. Pour into the pan and simmer gently over a low heat, whisking, for 10–15 minutes, or until the mixture thickens. Stir in the cajeta. Cool, then leave to stand in the refrigerator for 4 hours. Remove the vanilla pod, pour into paleta moulds and freeze for 2 hours. Add the lolly sticks and freeze for at least another 4 hours.

PALETAS DE JAMAICA

Hibiscus ice lollies

MAKES 6–8 ICE LOLLIES
1 litre/35fl oz/4⅓ cups water
35g/1¼oz/heaped 1 cup dried hibiscus flowers
150g/5½oz/¾ cup granulated sugar

1   Bring all the ingredients to the boil in a pan. Lower the heat and simmer gently for 30 minutes. Cool, then chill in the refrigerator for 4 hours. Strain off the flowers, pour into moulds and freeze for 2 hours. Add the lolly sticks and freeze for at least another 4 hours.

> **BUYER'S GUIDE TO PALETA MOULDS**
> Unless you want a lolly in the shape of a space ship or Olaf the snowman from *Frozen*, my advice is to buy proper 'paleta moulds' from Amazon. They cost about £10.

JAMONCILLO FRUTAS
GDE.
$ 240.00 Pza

CALAVERA # 9
$ 103.50 * Pza

CALAVERAS AZÚCAR
Sugar skulls

In southern Mexico there isn't a lot of money, so at some point in the 18th century the people began to make their religious decorations from what was available to them, namely sugar. Soon folk artists followed and also started to make sugar skulls to place on the family's ofrendas, altars, during Día de los Muertos (pages 150–157). Today, the skulls represent the spirits of passed-away relatives and their name is inscribed on the forehead to honour them and guide them home.

1　First get hold of the plastic moulds for making sugar skulls. Most moulds consist of a front and a back and they come in various shapes and sizes from places like mexicansugarskull. com. After that all you have to do is to mix together the granulated sugar and the egg whites until you have a snowball consistency. Pack it tightly into the moulds then, to make the skulls lighter, scoop out a little of the sugar with a spoon. Carefully turn the moulds over onto a lined baking sheet and repeat until you've got the desired number of skull halves. Preheat the oven to 110°C/225°F/gas ¼ and put your skulls in for 30 minutes to harden. Leave them in a dry place for 2–7 days until they feel hard, dry and completely stable.

2　It's time to make the icing. Check that your icing (confectioners') sugar does not contain cornflour (cornstarch). If it does, blend normal granulated sugar to a fine powder and use that instead. Super-easy. Now whisk the egg white and distilled vinegar with an electric whisk, then gradually add a little sugar at a time until you end up with something resembling a super-hard meringue. Divide the icing between plates – one plate per colour – and add the food colouring. Save a batch of uncoloured icing. If you want proper intense colours, mexicansugarskull.com also stock genuine Mexican, probably radioactive, food colouring. Spoon the icing into piping bags for the finer details.

3　Stick the back and front of your sugar skulls together with the uncoloured icing. Wait for 30 minutes until it has dried. Then just let yourself be inspired by the pictures in this book and decorate away. Give the finished sugar skulls as gifts, use them to decorate the home, as place cards or just for summoning the spirits of the dead when the gateway to the underworld opens on the next Día de los muertos.

MAKES 6–12 SKULLS
1kg/2lb 4oz/5½ cups granulated
　sugar
2 egg whites

Icing:
480g/1lb 1oz/scant 3½ cups icing
　(confectioners') sugar
1 egg white
1 tsp distilled vinegar (12%)
food colouring in various colours

PANELA DE TRES LECHES
Cake with three kinds of milk

Popular in many parts of South America, the Mexicans have a special place in their hearts for this sweet, wet, and crisp dessert, the origins of which are thought to be influenced by classic spirit-infused European desserts like British rum cake and Italian tiramisu – hence the dash of rum. If you like sweet things, visit Pasteleriá La Ideal in Mexico City – a traditional patisserie and a temple for those not afraid of developing a spare tyre (www.pastelerialaideal.com.mx).

1   Preheat the oven to 180°C/350°F/gas 4. Mix together the flour, baking powder and salt in a bowl. In another bowl, whisk together the egg yolks, the oil, the scraped-out vanilla pod and the water. Whisk the egg whites and add the sugar a little at a time until small peaks form. Turn it upside down over your head to check that you've whisked hard enough – that's a classic, and classics you don't mess around with. Carefully stir about one quarter of the egg whites into the yolks. Add one quarter of the flour and then another quarter of the whites. Continue until everything is mixed together. Pour the batter into a greased cake tin coated with breadcrumbs and bake in the middle of the oven for about 40 minutes until the cake has coloured and is baked through. Check with a cocktail stick to see if it's done. Remove from the oven and leave to cool.

2   For the tres leches, stir together the cream, sweetened condensed milk, evaporated milk and rum. If you want small individual cakes, use a cutter or a glass to cut out round shapes from the sponge. Otherwise you can leave it as a big cake, though it won't look as nice. Cut the sponge into two horizontally and pour the tres leches mixture over both halves so that the sponge gets all lovely and soaked. Leave to stand in the refrigerator for a while until it has set.

3   Toast the almonds in a hot dry frying pan until they've started to colour and smell nice. Whip the cream with the icing (confectioners') sugar. Spread some cream onto one half of the sponge. Place the other half on top and spread cream all over it. Press the toasted almonds onto the sides and the top and place a cocktail cherry in the middle. Beautiful!

SERVES 6

125g/4½oz/1 cup plain (all-purpose) flour
1½ tsp baking powder
1 pinch salt
4 eggs, separated
3 tbsp vegetable oil
1 vanilla pod
2 tbsp water
110g/3¾oz/scant ⅔ cup granulated sugar

Tres leches:
200ml/7fl oz/scant 1 cup whipping cream
200ml/7fl oz/scant 1 cup sweetened condensed milk
200ml/7fl oz/scant 1 cup evaporated milk or single cream
100ml/3½fl oz/scant ½ cup rum

Decoration:
100g/3½oz/¾ cup almond flakes
250ml/9fl oz/generous 1 cup whipping cream
50g/1¾oz/¾ cup icing (confectioners') sugar
cocktail cherries

CHOCOFLÁN IMPOSIBLE

Magic chocolate cake with crème brûlée

Imagine a cake that is half crème brûlée, half brownie and you start to get a feel for how special this classic Mexican cake is. But the magic isn't just in the taste, because during the baking, the brûlée and chocolate layers actually swap places!

---

1   Preheat the oven to 180°C/350°F/gas 4. Pour a little cajeta into a 20–25cm/8–10in cake tin. Stir together the dry ingredients (apart from the nuts) in a bowl. Scrape the seeds out of the vanilla pod. Melt the butter and whisk with the seeds, the buttermilk and the egg. Pour the wet ingredients into the dry ones and whisk into a smooth batter. Pour into the cake tin.

2   Whisk together the ingredients for the flan, apart from the vanilla pod, until they're just mixed. Scrape the seeds from the vanilla pod, add the seeds to the bowl and whisk a little more. Pour the mixture over the chocolate layer in the tin and place the tin a deep oven dish filled with warm water. Place in the middle of the oven and bake for about 1 hour. Take out the cake and note that the chocolate is now on top.

3   Leave to cool. Cut around the edge of the cake with a knife. Flip the tin over and if the cake doesn't come out straight away, dab the tin with some paper towels rinsed in warm water until you hear the cake plop out. Serve with lots of finely chopped pecan nuts on the top and some extra cajeta to drizzle over – because it tastes so amazing.

SERVES 6

cajeta (below) or dulce de leche
75g/2½oz/heaped ⅓ cup granulated sugar
75g/2½oz/heaped ⅓ cup plain (all-purpose) flour
40g/1½oz/⅓ cup cocoa powder
½ tsp bicarbonate of soda (baking soda)
½ tsp baking powder
½ vanilla pod
100g/3½oz butter
150ml/5fl oz/⅔ cup buttermilk
1 egg
90g/3oz/scant 1 cup pecan nuts

Flan:
400ml/14fl oz/1¾ cups single cream
400ml/14fl oz/1¾ cups condensed milk
4 eggs
½ vanilla pod
½ tsp salt

CAJETA   Traditional Mexican caramel sauce from goat's milk

1 litre/35fl oz/4⅔ cups goat's or cow's milk
190g/6¾oz/heaped 1 cup granulated sugar
1 tbsp glucose
1 pinch salt
1 vanilla pod
1 pinch bicarbonate of soda (baking soda)

Mix the milk, sugar, glucose and salt in a heavy-based pan. Scrape in the seeds from the vanilla pod. Bring to the boil, stirring, then remove from the heat and add the bicarbonate of soda (baking soda). Return to the heat and simmer very gently until the sauce is light brown, about 1 hour, stirring occasionally.

Happy churros bakers at the beautiful art deco churrería El Moro, in Mexico City. Unless you've got a deep-fryer that's several cubic metres in volume, you should probably not attempt making such enormous churros as these pros. But it's tempting, I know.

CHURROS CON CANELA
Piped deep-fried doughnuts with sugar and cinnamon

If you like less dough and more crunch, these are the doughnuts for you! This traditional Spanish pastry has been adopted by the Mexicans, who mainly eat it for breakfast with a cup of hot, home-roasted chocolate or café de olla. If you want to turn up the decadence a few notches you can, of course. serve it as a dessert with homemade chocolate or goat's milk caramel sauce.

1 Bring the water to the boil with the butter, salt and sugar. Mix in the flour and cook in the pan for 3 minutes over a medium heat until smooth. Transfer to a bowl and cool for a few minutes. Vigorously whisk in the egg until smooth.

2 Fill the piping bag with the dough. The dough will swell as you deep-fry it, so use a 5mm/¼in star-shaped nozzle, smaller than you might think; it will give you nice ridges on your churros. If you want, you can keep the piping bag in the refrigerator; the dough will keep perfectly for a day or so.

3 Mix the cinnamon and sugar on a plate. Heat the oil to about 180°C/350°F. If you haven't got a thermometer, the oil is ready when a lump of dough sizzles and falls to the bottom of the pan only to rise directly up to the top again. Squeeze out about 15cm/6in long churros, cut off with scissors and deep-fry until golden brown, turning once. Take out and place on paper towels to drain. Coat in cinnamon and sugar. Done! Now for the difficult bit: to choose whether to dip your churros into chocolate or caramel sauce or just drink the world's tastiest hot chocolate or coffee with them.

SERVES 6
350ml/12fl oz/1½ cups water
50g/1¾oz butter
½ tsp salt
1 tbsp granulated sugar
125g/4½oz/1 cup plain (all-purpose) flour
1 egg
1 tsp ground Ceylon or standard cinnamon
3 tbsp granulated sugar
oil for deep-frying

TO SERVE
chocolate caliente (see page 124) or salsa de chocolate (see page 124) or cajeta (see page 110) or café de olla (see below)

CAFÉ DE OLLA Spicy boiled coffee

SERVES 4
1 litre/35fl oz/4⅓ cups water
5 tbsp piloncillo or muscovado sugar
5cm/1¾in Ceylon or standard cinnamon stick
2 thumb-size pieces of orange zest
75g/2½oz/⅔ cup coarsely ground, dark coffee

This spicy Mexican coffee tastes amazing both with churros and on its own. Just bring the water to the boil. Add the sugar, cinnamon and zest and leave to simmer on a medium heat for 5 minutes. Add the coffee and leave to steep for a further 5 minutes. Strain and drink.

Churros with a cup of hot chocolate.

A sweet-toothed couple checks out the window at Mexico City's most beautiful sweet shop, Dulcería de Celaya.

BEBIDAS

A proper feast recipe for chocolate in Oaxaca: cocoa beans, sugar, almonds and Ceylon cinnamon.

TODO SOBRE EL CHOCOLATE

All about home-roasted chocolate

If you've never experienced the smell of freshly roasted cocoa beans that have been ground into a rich batter with almonds, sugar and cinnamon, immediately stop what you're doing and have a crack at the recipe on page 124. Home-roasted chocolate smells and tastes similar to standard chocolate, but with just a little something extra. It's earthier, richer, and spicier – tasting the first sample from the mixture feels a little bit like getting a head massage from Mother Earth (that's a good thing, trust me).

 would estimate that about 70 per cent of my happiest childhood memories involve a cup of steaming hot chocolate. My parents served it to me when we went skiing, when we went crayfish fishing, or with a sausage sandwich when I came home after swimming practice with icicles in my hair. Those with a sweet tooth really have a lot to thank Mexico for. The first vanilla pod, for example, was cultivated from wild orchids in Veracruz on the Mexican east coast in pre-Columbian times, and as early as the 1500s BC they drank the very first cup of hot chocolate in the same area. For Central America's Indians, the cocoa plant quickly became an incredibly important crop; the beans were used as currency and the drink was regarded as holy. They drank it during religious rituals, for virility and fertility and just because it was so damn delicious.

Still today it's more common to drink chocolate in Mexico than to eat it. And Mexican chocolate really is something else. In standard, industrial chocolate production, the cocoa powder is separated from the cocoa butter only to be mixed in again at a later point. It's then conched and tempered in an incredibly complicated process. In the small chocolate factories in the Mexican countryside they use an easier method: they simply throw the freshly roasted beans into a mill. If it's a special occasion, they may add a few nuts, some cinnamon and vanilla. The flavour isn't as refined as we're used to, but it has a raw, original quality that is completely lost in industry-produced chocolate. To drink a cup of Mexican chocolate for the first time is like getting a big, warm hug after a lifetime of perfunctory handshakes.

At the chocolate factory in the village of Zaachilla in Oaxaca, your chocolate is ground while you wait. Just pick your special blend, take it to the mill and a few minutes later you get the most aromatic, fresh and luxurious chocolate sauce that's ever been carried in a plastic bag.

TABLETAS DE CHOCOLATE

Home-roasted chocolate

MAKES ABOUT 20 CHUNKS

115g/4oz/2 cups almonds
10cm/4in Ceylon or standard cinnamon stick
250g/9oz raw cocoa beans or 200g/7oz cocoa nibs
300g/10½oz/1⅔ cups granulated sugar

1   Raw cocoa beans don't come straight from the tree, in case that's what you thought; instead they are fermented but left unroasted. Raw cacao nibs are cacao beans without their shell. Both can be found in health-food shops. You roast the beans for the flavour, but also to kill any bacteria that might have popped up during fermentation – so don't taste the beans first. Or have you already done that? Don't worry. I suppose. Preheat the oven to 180°C/350°F/gas 4 and start by roasting the almonds in the middle of the oven for 10 minutes and the cinnamon for 5 minutes. Lower the heat to 150°C/300°F/gas 2 and roast the raw cocoa beans for about 15–20 minutes until they've changed colour and the shells start to crack. Stir occasionally. Don't roast them for too long or they will go bitter. If you're using raw cocoa nibs, roast them for 10–15 minutes.

2   Once the beans have cooled, crush the thin shell between your palms and pick off and blow away the shells. It can take a while, so this might be when you regret not having bought the cocoa nibs. When you're done, put the shelled beans in a food processor or blender and chop them until they start to resemble chocolate sauce. This can take up to 30 minutes depending on your machine. First they get chopped, then they look like brown peanut butter and finally the oil separates out and you've got a thick sauce. Add the almonds, cinnamon and sugar and blend to a paste. It's okay if the sugar doesn't dissolve properly. We're talking drinking chocolate here, not eating chocolate. That takes even more effort to make.

3   Line an ovenproof dish with baking parchment. Pour in the chocolate and leave to set for a minute, then make a chequerboard pattern with a sharp knife dipped in hot water, scoring the chocolate into 2.5 x 5cm/1 x 1¾in chunks. Leave to set overnight. The next day, break into pieces and store in a jar. Voila! Now you've got lots of homemade chocolate chunks to use for hot chocolate, chocolate sauce or cooking. They are a bit too grainy to eat as they are – but you should, of course, try anyway. They will keep fresh for 2 months.

CHOCOLATE CALIENTE

Warm aromatic chocolate

MAKES 1 CUP

1 chunk of home-made chocolate (see above)
200ml/7fl oz/scant 1 cup milk

1   Grate the chocolate into the milk and heat slowly. Whisk vigorously so you get a nice froth. Add extra milk or chocolate if needed.

SALSA DE CHOCOLATE

Spicy chocolate sauce

SERVES 4

4 chunks of homemade chocolate (see above)
100ml/3½fl oz/scant ½ cup whipping cream

1   Grate the chocolate into the cream. Heat slowly while stirring constantly and you will end up with a creamy, spicy sauce. The world's tastiest – guaranteed. Eat with ice cream, churros or anything else you fancy eating with chocolate sauce.

AGUAS FRESCAS

Fresh, natural and super-refreshing fruit beverages

Agua fresca actually means fresh water, and that's just what these beverages are: fresh, natural, water-based drinks that are super thirst-quenching loaded with ice on a hot day. Everywhere in Mexico you'll find small fruit stalls and juice places that sell these six classics, and lots and lots more. And even though there are chia seeds in one of the recipes, the others are free from kale and celery as well as fennel and wheatgrass – I guarantee it.

AGUA DE TAMARINDO

Fresh tamarind cordial

SERVES 10

20 tamarind pods
2 litres/70fl oz/8 cups water
250g/9oz/heaped 1⅓ cups granulated sugar
ice

1   You'll find tamarind in Asian food stores; it looks as though a kiwi had a child with a green bean. It mostly consists of hard shell and seeds surrounded by a brown paste that is used for cooking in India and Asia, as well as for making Worcestershire sauce. In Mexico it's a common sweet flavour. To make tamarind cordial, you peel off the hard shell and then you pop the rest in a pan together with the water and the sugar. Bring to the boil, lower the heat and leave to simmer for 30 minutes without a lid. Turn off the heat and leave to cool for about 4 hours.

2   Take out the tamarind, pick out the seeds and throw them away. Put the gooey fruit flesh back into the water. Blend the flesh and the water, run through a sieve and pour into nice glass bottles. When you fancy a glass of agua de tamarindo, you simply fill a glass with ice, pour over some tamarind cordial and dilute with water until it's the right strength.

AGUA DE MELÓN

Fresh melon drink

SERVES 10

1 ripe honeydew or cantaloupe melon
500ml/17fl oz/2 cups water
2 tbsp granulated sugar.
1 tbsp freshly squeezed lime juice
ice

1   Peel the melon and chop the flesh. Blend with the water, sugar and lime juice until smooth. Since all melons vary in sweetness, add more water, sugar or lime to taste. Strain through muslin (cheesecloth). Check the flavour again and chill. Fill a glass with ice and add melon drink to enjoy something refreshing.

AGUA DE JAMAICA

Fresh hibiscus cordial

SERVES 10

2 litres/70fl oz/8 cups water
250g/9oz/heaped 1⅓ cups granulated sugar
125g/4½oz/4 cups dried hibiscus flowers
2 tbsp freshly squeezed lime juice
ice

1   You can find dried hibiscus flowers in tea shops, and they are jam-packed with antioxidants to lower your blood pressure.

But above all they have an amazingly fresh flavour and in Mexico they are crazy for it. To prepare the cordial, boil the water and sugar and add the hibiscus flowers. Lower the heat and simmer gently for 30 minutes without a lid. Leave to cool for about 4 hours.

2   Strain off the flowers, add the lime juice and pour into bottles. When you fancy a drink, fill a glass with ice, pour over the hibiscus cordial and dilute until it's the right strength.

AGUA DE LIMÓN

Fresh lime cordial

SERVES 10

12 lime
2 litres/70fl oz/8 cups water
375g/13oz/heaped 2 cups granulated sugar
ice

1   Zest the limes and leave the zest to steep in the water in a pan for 1 hour. Add the sugar, bring to the boil and simmer gently for 30 minutes without a lid. Squeeze in the juice of 6 limes and leave to cool completely, for at least 4 hours. Strain off the lime zest and pour into glass bottles. Fill a glass with ice, pour over lime cordial and dilute with water until you've got the right strength.

HORCHATA

Cinnamon-flavoured rice milk

SERVES 6

200g/7oz/heaped 1 cup long-grain rice
5cm/1¾in Ceylon or standard cinnamon stick
500ml//17fl oz/2 cups almond milk
1 vanilla pod
180g/6¼oz/1 cup granulated sugar
ice

1   Some might find this Christmassy porridge-tasting rice drink a tad unusual. The first

time I drank horchata I thought it tasted like diluted face cream. Nowadays I love it, of course. Here's how to make it. Toast the uncooked rice and cinnamon in a hot dry frying pan for about 2 minutes until coloured. Blend to a fine powder, add the almond milk and the seeds from the vanilla pod and stir. Leave in the refrigerator overnight and then sieve through muslin (cheesecloth). Squeeze out the last remaining drop. Add the sugar and stir until dissolved. Pour over ice and take a big gulp. Mmm – face cream.

2   You can also use the horchata to make the world's best iced-coffee drink. Add loads of freshly ground coffee to a filter. Place over a jug with ice. Pour boiling water over the coffee and let it filter through and cool over the ice. Top up with horchata and add more ice, if needed.

CHIA FRESCO

Mexican lemonade with chia seeds

SERVES 8

3 cucumbers
1.5 litres/52fl oz/6 cups water
150g/5½oz/¾ cup granulated sugar
200ml/7fl oz/1 cup freshly squeezed lime juice
2 tbsp chia seeds
ice

1   Chia seeds were ascribed almost supernatural qualities in Christopher McDougall's *Born to Run* and have now been almost completely adopted by the juicing fanatics. But in Mexico this lemonade is not only drunk because it's good for intestinal cleansing, but also because it's tasty – in a bit of a slimy, crisp way. To make, blend the cucumbers, water and sugar, then sieve. Add the lime juice, adjusting the flavour, if needed, then add the chia seeds. Chill for 15 minutes, then serve with ice.

TEPACHE

Home-brewed pineapple beer

Are you having issues getting people to drink your slightly too cloudy, over-hopped, home-brewed IPA? You should try brewing this ridiculously simple fermented pineapple beer instead. Everyone will love it, from beer nerds to non-drinkers. Because tepache is a low-alcohol pineapple beer that isn't only incredibly thirst-quenching drunk with a lot of ice on a hot summer's day; it's also a perfect base for both micheladas and mezcal and tequila cocktails.

TEPACHE

Home-brewed pineapple beer

SERVES 10

4 litres/140fl oz/17 cups water
450g/1lb piloncillo (see page 27), or equal
    amounts of muscovado and granulated sugar
10cm/4in Ceylon or standard cinnamon stick
4 cloves
1 ripe organic pineapple
1 bottle (33cl) Mexican lager

1   Bring the water to the boil with the sugar, cinnamon and cloves until the sugar has dissolved. Leave to simmer for 10 minutes then turn off the heat and leave to cool down completely. Remove the leaves from the pineapple. You can rinse the pineapple first, but as the natural yeast sits on the peel, don't scrub it. Cut the unpeeled pineapple into cubes and add to a fermentation bucket or large jug with the sugar syrup. Cover with a piece of fabric so you don't get any flies in it but the beverage can breathe.

2   Leave to ferment for 1–2 days in a warm place. When it has started to fizz lightly, sniff it. If it smells like sausages or vinegar, something has gone wrong and you can throw the lot away. But if it has a deep, sweet, spicy pineapple smell, the tepache is on

its way, so pour in the beer to speed up the fermentation. Leave to ferment for 12 hours maximum; any longer and there's a big chance the tepache will turn to vinegar.

3   Strain the drink thoroughly and pour into a jug that fits in the refrigerator. Tepache normally has an alcohol content of 1–5 per cent and is not only incredibly refreshing, but is jam-packed with good stuff from the fermentation process. Enjoy it on its own, as a tepachelada or as a mixer with a dash of lime, ice and mezcal or tequila.

TEPACHELADA

Tepache beer drink

MAKES 1 DRINK

1 lime wedge
120ml/4fl oz/½ cup tepache (see recipe above)
1 tsp chilli sauce, such as Cholula
1 bottle (33cl) Mexican lager
salt, tajín (see page 27) or sal de gusano
    (see page 17)
ice

1   Homemade pineapple beer topped with more beer – what could be better? Run the lime around the edge of a beer glass and dip into a plate filled with salt. Pour in the tepache and chilli sauce, add ice and top up with beer.

MICHELADAS

Three kinds of refreshing, super-spicy-salty beer-based cocktails

The name of these incredibly popular beer-based cocktails is said to derive from the expression 'mi chela helada', which means 'my ice-cold beer'. As well as being an affectionate nickname, it's also a hint to how the drinks should be served. There are (almost) as many michelada recipes as there are Mexicans and both the name and the ingredients vary depending on which area you're in. They do have one thing in common though: I want to drink them all.

MICHELADA

Beer cocktail with spicy tomato juice

MAKES 1 DRINK

1 lime wedge
salt, tajín (see page 27) or sal de gusano (see page 17)
1 tbsp freshly squeezed lime juice
100ml/3½fl oz/scant ½ cup tomato juice
1 tsp Maggi or celery salt
1 tsp Worcestershire sauce
1 tsp tabasco
1 bottle (33cl) Mexican lager
ice

1   The classic michelada could be described as a Bloody Mary light, with beer instead of vodka. Run the lime around the edge of a glass and dip in a plate of salt. Pour in all the ingredients apart from the beer, add ice and top up with beer. Drink with a shot of mezcal. For a darker, fuller version, replace the lager with dark Mexican beer and the tomato juice with clamato – tomato and mussel juice.

CHAMOYELADA

Beer cocktail with chamoy sauce

MAKES 1 DRINK

1 tbsp + a bit extra chamoy sauce (see page 27)
2 tbsp + a bit extra tajín (see page 27)
1 tsp chilli sauce, such as Cholula

2 tbsp freshly squeezed lime juice
100ml/3½fl oz/scant ½ cup mango juice
1 bottle (33cl) Mexican lager
chamoy stick (see page 17) (optional)
ice

1   Mix 1 tbsp each chamoy sauce and tajín on a plate. Pour tajín only onto another. Dip the edge of a beer glass first into the mixture, then into the tajín. Add the chilli sauce, 1 tbsp chamoy and the lime and mango juice. Add ice and top up with beer. Add a chamoy stick (see page 17) if you can find one, of course.

LAGERITA

Lager + margarita = lagerita

MAKES 1 DRINK

1 lime wedge
salt, tajín (see page 27) or sal de gusano (see page 17)
1 margarita (see page 139)
1 bottle (33cl) Mexican lager
ice

1   Run the lime around the edge of a beer glass and dip the glass in salt. Pour in your margarita. Add ice, then the beer, with the bottle standing upside-down in the glass. The beer will slowly trickle out as you drink. Genius. But do use a straw unless you want the bottle in your face.

MARGARITAS Y PALOMA

Mexico's two most classic cocktails

No one knows whether the margarita was invented in Mexico or in the US, but even if the popular cocktail's origins remain a mystery, there is no question that it is now fully ingrained in Mexican drinks culture. The only cocktail that threatens its status as Mexico's national drink numero uno would be the paloma, which could be described as a Central American tequila version of the Swedish 'Grappo vodka'. I like to make it with fresh grapefruit juice.

MARGARITA

Classic margarita

MAKES 1 DRINK

1 lime wedge
3 tbsp blanco tequila
2 tbsp cointreau
2 tbsp freshly squeezed lime juice
1½ tbsp agave syrup
fine salt
ice
lime slice

1 Run a lime wedge around the edge of a tumbler or a fancy glass on a foot. Dip the glass in fine salt. Measure all the ingredients in a shaker, add ice and shake. Sieve into the glass and add a lime wheel for a nice finishing touch.

TOMMY'S MARGARITA

Margarita with agave syrup

MAKES 1 DRINK

1 lime wedge
4 tbsp blanco tequila
2 tbsp freshly squeezed lime juice
1½ tbsp agave syrup
lime wedge
salt
ice

1 A minimalistic margarita if you like a purer tequila flavour (or have forgotten to buy triple sec). Run a lime wedge around the edge of a tumbler or a fancy glass on a foot. Dip the glass in salt. Measure all the ingredients in a shaker, add ice and shake. Sieve into the glass but skip the lime wheel. This drink is far too hardcore for such nonsense.

PALOMA

Refreshing grapefruit cocktail

MAKES 1 DRINK

4 tbsp blanco tequila
2 tbsp agave syrup
1½ tbsp freshly squeezed lime juice
4 tbsp freshly squeezed grapefruit juice
ice
soda water

1 Pour the tequila and agave syrup into a tall Collins glass. Add the juices and stir. Add plenty of ice and top up with soda water.

> **BUYER'S GUIDE TO TEQUILA** Always choose a tequila that contains 100 per cent agave – the mixto is pretty much just agave-flavoured vodka. Not good. Also avoid novelty tequilas, with sombrero corks and so on. The blanco is the one usually used for cocktails, but an aged reposado works too.

TODO SOBRE EL MEZCAL

Everything about mezcal

Agave plants waiting to be roasted outside a mezcal distillery in the town of Matatlán in Oaxaca. In this area they produce more mezcal than anywhere else in Mexico.

The roasted agave is crushed in a stone mill, then comes fermentation and finally distillation. Yes!

Even though mezcal cocktails can be amazing, I thought we should learn to drink it like the Mexicans: straight. But there are a few things to keep in mind if you want the ultimate mezcal experience and get as well-oiled as a malaria-infected British consul donning a wrinkly linen suit. Here is a crash course in the art of drinking mezcal the Mexican way.

Buy a good-quality mezcal
While tequila is made in factories, under strict regulations and from blue agave, mezcal is a pure artisan product that can be made from any of 100 different kinds of agave, which gets its smoky flavour from being roasted in the ground. Just like wine, it's also affected by its terroir – the ground it's growing in, the weather that surrounds it and the people who produce it. So mezcal could either taste like the nectar of the Aztec gods or, as Malcolm Lowry describes it in *Under the Volcano*, 'like 10 yards of barbed wire'.

Choose the right glass In bars, mezcal is served in a shot glass, a cognac snifter or a veladora – a burned out grave-candle glass (see page 17). Jicaras (on the right) are cups beautifully carved from the bark of the jicaras tree. If you want to drink like a Zapotec Indian then get a clay bowl, a copita, and make a toast with a resounding 'stigibeu!' – 'to the life force that is around us!'

Nibble Dried figs, grasshoppers and tacos all go well with mezcal, but the most common, and tastiest, snack is orange slices sprinkled with sal de gusano (see page 17). Sal de gusano is made of salt, chilli and ground maguey worms – not as strange as it sounds because the worms actually live in the agave plant, so they have already flavoured the spirit. That's why you see worms in mezcal bottles, although that's more of a tourist thing.

Drink in the right way In Mexico they say mezcal shouldn't be downed, it should be kissed – so sip it slowly. Mezcal also goes brilliantly with food. The earthy flavour marries with all kinds of masa, and the salty and sour with chilli-hot food. The absolutely most important thing, however, is that mezcal is a spirit that is meant to be shared. So for the ultimate mezcal experience, go out and sit in the sun with friends. Open a bottle of mezcal. Put on some music. Dip some orange in sal de gusano. Sip. Laugh. Feel the life force that's around you.

Ready for another mezcal? – bring it on!

DÍA DE LOS
MUERTOS

PART 6: THREE DAYS AT THE FESTIVAL OF THE DEAD IN OAXACA

It is Tuesday 4th November and I'm sitting on my suitcase in Mexico City's Aeropuerto Internacional waiting for my flight to be called. I try to focus on the last lines of Malcolm Lowry's classic novel *Under the Volcano*, but the text gets blurred by all the thoughts that keep popping into my head. Because visiting Mexico is to get one's head so stuffed with sights, sounds and sensations that it feels like someone has tried to squeeze a sleeping bag into it. In the last few days I've eaten more and better street food than anywhere in the world. I've eaten tacos, gorditas and tlacoyos, grasshoppers, worms and powdered ants. I've drunk micheladas and strolled around mercados as big as city districts. I've been offered mezcal by a grave in Oaxaca at midnight, have had fireworks explode no more than a fist's distance away from my head and seen zombie-painted adults scare three-year-olds with such relish that it would leave a Western child bedridden. I've seen marigolds in the shade of traffic cones and a donkey dragging a cart filled with sugar cane. I've made a pilgrimage to Frida Kahlo's kitchen, drunk spirits that taste of chicken fillets and eaten fruit that looked like lime but tasted like orange. I've had a visitation from the dead.

※ ※ ※

I've also, I realize, fulfilled an old dream. Even since the first time I read the book I'm now struggling to finish again, I've dreamt about celebrating Día de los Muertos in Oaxaca. You see, *Under the Volcano* tells the story of a British consul who is torn between love and alcohol during Día de los Muertos in a village outside Oaxaca in 1938.

※ ※ ※

The festival is thought to go back over 3,000 years. When the Spanish conquistadors came to Mexico 500 years ago they found the locals celebrating an ancient festival in which they seemed to challenge death. They ate, drank, partied and carried skulls and pictures of the death goddess, Mictecacihuatl. They did their utmost to show they had the cojones to face up to death.

※ ※ ※

In contrast to the Christian Spaniards, the Indians regarded life as a dream, and believed that you didn't finally wake up until you died. And these old rituals didn't quite vanish. Before long they had melded with the Catholic traditions, were assimilated with All Saints' Day and soon became Día de los Muertos. Today it's the biggest religious festival in Mexico, or at least in the south, which is still characterized more by the Indian culture. On 31st October, they celebrate the Día de angelitos, the day of the little angels. At midnight, the souls of dead children return to unite with their families for 24 hours.

※ ※ ※

The next day it's the adult relatives' turn to return to earth, and on the 2nd November all souls are allowed to return at the same time.

On the 28th day of each month you can see people carrying around statues depicting St Jude, the patron saint of lost causes.

> '**The fundamental idea behind the celebrations is that the dead would be offended by being remembered with sadness and would rather have a party.**'

The fundamental idea behind the celebrations is that the dead would be offended by being remembered with sadness and would rather have a party on their yearly return to earth. That's why the dead are celebrated with food, music, mezcal and all the other things that the late relatives enjoyed while still alive.

❋ ❋ ❋

Altars, ofrendas, and homes are decorated and set up for a feast with mole negro, pan de muerto, home-ground chocolate, orange, lime, bananas, nuts and incense. In the towns they organize parades where people paint their faces like skulls – calaveras – and sit on relatives' graves to eat, drink, laugh and remember.

I am sitting in my hotel room waiting for it to get late enough to visit one of these graveyards when something strange occurs. I swear this is completely true. Exactly when the clock strikes midnight, just when the gates to the underworld open, according to the folklore, the door to my room suddenly flies open and an ice-cold gust of wind whips its way through the room and up my spine, only to quickly rush out again. Shaken, I down a glass of mezcal and go out onto the streets.

❋ ❋ ❋

In the enormous graveyard, Panteón General, in central Oaxaca, it looks like a music festival directed by Tim Burton. Thousands of skeleton-painted people eat tacos and chicharrones from a street food stall, listen to mariachi music and drink hot chocolate spiked with mezcal. By the graves, people sit and have picnics.

❋ ❋ ❋

The morning after, I visit a graveyard in one of the small Indian villages outside Oaxaca. Everywhere, small fires are smouldering where the grave candles have set alight the marigold bouquets that are piled by the graves, and there's a smoky mist lingering over the whole place. Scattered around the graves are empty mezcal and tequila bottles, and on newspapers and pieces of cardboard you can clearly see the outlines of sleeping bodies. Despite it looking more like a gang of grave robbers gone berserk than the aftermath of a religious festival, it's incredibly beautiful. I think about how fundamentally different this attitude towards death is in comparison to that in the West.

'Scattered around the graves are empty mezcal and tequila bottles, and on newspapers and pieces of cardboard you can clearly see the outlines of sleeping bodies.'

I remember how terribly cold, stiff and scary I thought it was when, as a child, I had to go to a graveyard and put flowers on a relative's grave. I had to be completely quiet, collected and solemn, and if I made the smallest of disturbances to the carefully raked gravel path, I immediately got an icy stare from one of my elderly relatives. I was so scared of doing anything inappropriate that I convinced myself that if I accidentally trod on a grave a mummified hand would burst from the ground and pull me down. The thought of death on the whole is something that our culture has rationalized away and that we do our best to avoid. But when we, from time to time, happen to catch a glimpse of it from the corner of our eyes it leaves us paralysed with fear. So am I also supposed to die? To me, this sounds completely unreasonable and old-fashioned.

❊ ❊ ❊

During Día de los Muertos, on the other hand, you don't deny the inevitable but face it head on. 'I'm not scared of you', is what you say, and 'I know you'll come one day. But right now I'm alive and so I will eat, sing and drink so much mezcal that I fall asleep next to the grave of someone who isn't as lucky to be alive'. As a result, the knowledge that one day you will lie in the ground of a Mexican graveyard doesn't feel cold, stiff and scary – but beautiful, warm and oddly appealing. If you grow up around here, I think, you are less scared of death.

❊ ❊ ❊

And, as a consequence, also of life? I sit on my suitcase at Mexico City's Aeropuerto Internacional and wait for my flight to be called. I take a deep breath and force myself to finish the book. 'No se puede vivir sin amar' – 'you can't live without loving' – the consul thinks as he plummets down into the volcano at the end. The last thing he sees, however, is that someone throws in a dead dog after him. I let out a laugh, close the book and hear my flight being called.

❊ ❊ ❊

I walk to the gate and think how strange it is when things that you thought would be life-changing actually turn out to be so. I feel a touch of fear of flying but think that when the inevitable happens at last, all I have to do is to give a big smile and show my cojones. Then I board the plane.

RECITE LIST

First published in the United Kingdom in 2016 by
Pavilion
43 Great Ormond Street
London
WC1N 3HZ

Copyright © Jonas Cramby
Natur & Kultur, Stockholm

ISBN 978-1-91090-431-2

A CIP catalogue record for this book is available from the British Library.

10 9 8 7 6 5 4 3

Reproduction by Mission Productions Ltd, Hong Kong
Printed by Toppan Leefung Printing Ltd, China

This book can be ordered direct from the publisher at www.pavilionbooks.com

Photography: Calle Stoltz
Cover illustration: Charles Glaubitz
Design: Jonas Cramby
Editor: Maria Nilsson

The publisher would like to thank Frida Green for her work on this book.